T0062443

Mock Two

Ron Oliver

Laura Windisch, Cover Artist
Kore Oliver, Editor

Order this book online at www.trafford.com
or email orders@trafford.com

Most Trafford titles are also available at major online book retailers.

© Copyright 2010 Ron Oliver.
All rights reserved. No part of this publication may be reproduced, stored in a retrieval system, or transmitted, in any form or by any means, electronic, mechanical, photocopying, recording, or otherwise, without the written prior permission of the author.

Everything in this book is true. Some names and events have been changed to protect privacy.

Printed in Victoria, BC, Canada.

ISBN: 978-1-4269-2221-3 (sc)

ISBN: 978-1-4269-2222-0 (dj)

Library of Congress Control Number: 2009912294

Our mission is to efficiently provide the world's finest, most comprehensive book publishing service, enabling every author to experience success. To find out how to publish your book, your way, and have it available worldwide, visit us online at www.trafford.com

Trafford rev. 5/13/2010

 www.trafford.com

North America & international
toll-free: 1 888 232 4444 (USA & Canada)
phone: 250 383 6864 ♦ fax: 812 355 4082

ACKNOWLEDGEMENTS

This is dedicated to my children Kore and Zachary, my girlfriend Marilyn Milligan, the brilliant Beryt Oliver, my post Air Force flying buddy Fred Padula, and his mate Corinne Masri, and everyone else who may have helped me, including the B & B Lounge in Healdsburg, CA for 86ing me for life which gave me more time to finish this book. I'd personally like to thank them but they won't let me enter. Also, my old Air Force buddy John Dietrich who rescued me from the ghetto and helped me buy my cabin.

Finally to my Mom and Dad who endured long separations during WWII and the Korean War.

And then had their middle son go off to fight in Vietnam.

Dedication

I had much help and encouragement from many on this book, but the most in every way was Kore Oliver. She was editor, organizer, encourager, placater, and loving daughter.
Thanks for choosing me as your Dad when you reincarnated, Kore. You are the greatest.

"Might this not be considered a normal reaction of human nature, this anxiety for one's own life? Pilots fair better in this respect than the crewmembers because they are so preoccupied with the many things necessary to fly their airplanes. It seems that the other crewmembers are unable to sit idly by as the bomber thunders in toward the enemy, flying right into the spitting orange and red flashes of his gun muzzles. They must have something to do, to occupy themselves, or their fear may become overpowering."

ZERO!
By Masatake Okumiya and Jiro Horiskoshi with Martin Caidin

Contents

1. Day One Dance — 1
2. Fighter History — 7
3. Buzz's Song — 11
4. After Buzz, Back to Westerly — 16
5. Maids Mourn — 19
6. Crash to the Right — 20
7. Crash to the Right Hangover — 28
8. River Mines — 31
9. Seventy-Two Big Ones — 39
10. Biggest Asshole in the Squadron — 46
11. Converting Counters for Fun and Survival — 53
12. Gil's Bloody Short Run — 57
13. Bond and the Boys — 64
14. Kromer Delivers a Eulogy — 67
15. Save Your Ass Club — 69
16. Everyone's a Backseater — 74
17. The Broken Lance — 75
18. The Day the Chief Went Down — 81
19. Rocket and the Monk — 89
20. Rocket Attack — 92
21. Kelley Mahoney — 95
22. Road Cutting Raga — 100
23. Khe Sahn Smoke Screen — 104
24. Circling, Circling, Circling — 111

25. Hunger Grows   113

26. The Last Ride: Not with a Whimper but a Bang   118

27. Training and Alienation   121

28. Me and Tony Fight Buddy   126

29. Range Wars   130

30. Bach's Greatest Fallacy   137

31. Billy's Story   139

32. The Justice of it All   149

33. Glossary   157

Poetry

1.	Squirrels	xii
2.	Squatting	45
3.	F-4 Night Flight- with all due respect to Richard Bach and Antoine St' Exupery	51
4.	The only king is the cashiers ring (for Wallace Stevens)	52
5.	The officers club at Da Nang at dawn.	56
6.	Mechanics	72
7.	On a friend getting hit over A Shau Valley, punching out and calling in a strike on his own head	73
8.	On vacationing with a Chinese lady of the night in the middle of war	80
9.	To the Mig 15	88
10.	Sammy Martin thrice descends	98
11.	Uncle James – 1953	102
12.	Rites Rites Rites	120
13.	One day chasing Buddy	129
14.	On crashing a Beechcraft Bonanza alone	136
15.	To John Gillespie McGee	153

Squirrels

Squirrels remind me

Cutting nuts in hickory tree

Shotgun raised warm fur-blast

Brother smile grandpa grin

Next time I fire was at the Viet Minh

CHAPTER 1

Day One Dance

The first thing I always saw was the bombs. Some I liked. Some I hated. They all scared the shit out of me. I liked the five hundred pound ones; they were sleek with copper noses and cylindrical tails. The 750s I hated; those bulky bastards weren't right for the Phantom. They would resist the speed I wanted to go, because you see, I FUCKIN' WANTED TO GO FAST! They were bulbous, the 750s, and made for bombers, but then they had made the McDonnell Douglas F-4C a bomber-the best air combat machine in the world turned into a platform to kill things on the ground.

Welcome to god-cursed Da Nang in the late summer '67.

The wing with the most Mig kills in the great summer air battles of '67 had suffered great ignominy when a cong team had sneaked in close enough to get a 122mm rocket into a parked F-4. This caused a chain reaction that wiped out 20 Phantoms, a hell of an explosion even by Da Nang standards.

But who cared?

The great money machine can make more and more, but that takes time and in the meanwhile the great general in Saigon has decreed,

"You gentlemen in country will now leave the glorious strikes in Hanoi to the pampered wings in Americanized Thailand. I have for you the dirt work. You will strike in the southern part of North Vietnam. Day and night, you will hunt trucks, hunt guns, hunt more trucks. You will go to Laos, too. Here the Ho Chi Minh trail weaves through mountains and passes, river valleys, and jungle. Here, too, you will strike day and night. You will also fly close air support in the south, sometimes within sight of your own beloved field. These missions will serve to save our gloriously equipped but befuddled ground forces.

"Read well these words for you who fly and die can never expect to see me in person. Modern generals have too much to do to actually go into the field and talk to the warriors. Know that I raise my glass to your service."

Well, maybe he didn't say the last part but it fits, believe me.

This passage with embellishments was read on our first day by the second in command Wing Operations Officer who then gave this speech;

"The loss of our aircraft on the ground caused the general to give us these missions and take away Hanoi PAC Six strikes. And these dirty missions we will do. And when we stop the trucks the general will give back the glory."

The colonel looks dreamily over our heads. He intones about a PAC Six mission.

"Picture this: 80 airplanes all under one leader heading for Hanoi. There were 40 F-4s and 40 105s, all heavily laden. We, the F-4s, fly higher, for not only are we going to bomb; we are going to cover the Thuds from Migs. Near the border there will be tankers waiting for us, ten KC-135s ready to refuel eight fighters each. The refueling is magnificent, gentleman; you cannot help but be proud of the awesome elements in these operations. After we load up with fuel we hit the north and everyone can feel the excitement, the speed picking up as we near the target: Hanoi. Anti-aircraft is there, but mostly exploding below our altitude. When the Sams fire we can jam with this great new gear provided by our industry."

I look around the room the colonel has chosen to preach in, and it's bizarre. All the walls are painted, rather well, with war scenes. Lots of cumulonimbus clouds, the pretty summer fair weather ones, with F-4s diving through them. Exploding shells and tracers were everywhere.

'They looked to be strange with flowers bursting into fierce bloom.'

Steven Crane's *Red Badge of Courage* was still relevant.

There's a Mig being shot down on the wall behind the colonel and to my left a North Vietnamese industrial complex is burning away. The flak bursts are real nice: orange, red and yellow. Later, I would find that flak in the air had a dirty quality about it, looking actually like debris. When you think about it, that's what it was. Sky debris. Flug Alsweht Kanoue. Germans invented the term in WWII.

The colonel continues.

"When the entire fleet rolls in for the pass, you have 80 planes hurtling for the target…gentlemen…this is when you earn your pay. This is when you forget the danger; those 15 seconds are for the Air Force. There's no pulling off early, no shirking, you dive until the release point and trigger and then you pull 6 g's and head for the coast. And if you are really lucky maybe a Mig will try you out. Maybe you will get a chance to show those Russian trained bastards who the best really is…"

These 15 seconds are for the Air Force? Seems to me my whole weird-ass life is for the damn Air Force.

Steve Monague leans over and says,

"We don't have to do that shit. Cool."

I agree. It sounds good to me if we stay out of PAC Six and skip the Sams and the Migs and the biggest guns. If the colonel wants to kill a Mig or two, that's his problem. Oh, wait, he's wrapping up.

"This wing can stop the trucks. We will hunt and find and destroy everything in PAC One worth killing. Like our general said, our mission will be tough and dirty, all weather and all the time. This wing had the best flying when we were going to PAC Six, when we were getting more Migs than anyone and we were flying close air in South Vietnam which the Thailand bases cannot do by treaty. They are forbidden to fly air support in South Vietnam. We had the most diverse mandate of any strike wing from in country to Laos to PAC One and PAC Six. We're going to get Hanoi back. We're going to get Hanoi back. Welcome to the war, gentlemen."

I'm thinking, wait a minute, if we stop their trucks can't they just make more?

Still, Monague and I are well pleased with this news.

"The old Colonel wants to kill Migs. Fuck his Migs. This should be safer. There aren't many Sams in PAC One either. God bless the general. I've always loved generals." Steve laughs.

But he didn't laugh for long. We're sent to the Wing Commander.

The first compelling feature was the genuine cheerfulness of the wing commander; joie de vivre tingling off this guy. It was Jack LaLanne hardiness.

"Gentleman, you can't imagine the fun to be had here. I'm in charge of 26 different support units. Every one of them dedicated to our 90 Phantoms and crews."

"I'd still rather be in Europe," Steve whispers.

We were the only two guys on our McDill Air Force F-4 training class that had expressed a desire to go to Germany over this glorious opportunity facing us.

It went like this.

100 aircrew members were gathered in Tampa in a big room and some wiseass major asked who wanted to go to Vietnam. 98 guys raised their hands. Then they asked who wanted to go to

Europe. Steve and I alone raised our hands. Everyone stared at us while the wiseass says,

"That's too bad, you're all going to Vietnam. Just wanted to see who the weenies were."

A laugh rolled through the room.

But Europe still sounded good to me.

So now, here we were in Vietnam. They had given us the same room and we headed there to lay the bags down, bounce on the beds and then go drink. As we approached the building there was a smiling guy in a bathrobe and shower clogs coming out the door.

"Gentleman, welcome to Paradise. My name's Pete Johnson and I'm leaving this dark realm for the boredom of pilot training instructor."

Immediately likable, we wished him the best.

Montague says, "Hey, that's a good sign. The guy made it through. Let's dump bags and go bar hopping."

I was feeling pretty good myself. The room was cool because aircrews have the only air conditioning on base. Steve won the flip and I got the top bunk, climbed up, leaned over, and looked down at my roomie, when the room exploded with the sound of HELL! It was tenaciously loud. The sound hurt me as much as it scared me. I hit the floor trying to imagine. Then, from the hallway someone yelled for a medic. Steve and I crawled to the door and looked out, to see a guy with a first aid kit running out the front door. I lay impotent, looking, when a different guy came back in the door head down, looked at us and said,

"They got Johnson. He gets though the whole fucking thing and they get him on the way to the shower. He was leaving in the morning."

Steve asks if it was a sapper or a bomber.

"No, man it was a 122 millimeter rocket; they shoot them all the time, trying to hit this building. Killing pilots is a big game, even on the ground. You guys just got here? Good fucking luck.

I got nine more North, then, if they don't blow me up, it's out of this hole."

Steve went outside to look. I stayed in the room, unable to move, unable to comprehend. The sound seemed to echo through the walls. I just couldn't get up and go look at that kind of pain. I couldn't. I just lay still when suddenly there was a siren wail and Steve came in, stricken.

"He's dead, man. It's unbelievable."

30 seconds later, one more rap by the colonel, one more grasping for luggage, one more pause, and it would have, could have been Steve and me. Four years of Air Force Academy, a year and a half of pilot training and we could be lying there shattered. This is taking blindless chance way too far.

We went for the first drink, cognizant of the fact we hadn't yet seen the flight line.

CHAPTER 2

Fighter History

At Da Nang an F-4 squadron's backseaters, and frontseaters too, had a strange kind of pecking order. It was based on how many missions north had been flown. Unlike WWII, where a large crew flew together through their missions, here it was constantly changing. True, everyone had an officially named counterpart, like my frontseater Hank Westerly. But it was also true that this relationship had many variables.

Time showed a different color, a different shade. A guy with 80 North had an investment, knowledge, and a power over time. He breathed the air of one of the 80 percent saved. Those with fewer missions truthfully stood in the shadow of such true riches, such real wisdom.

And, like all combat, if you survived the early part of your tour the odds improved. Not just because of the fewer missions to go, but because you got smarter. Like a good defensive boxer, you should get harder to hit.

The dynamic of the two seats had another angle. Never before in the history of combat aircraft had the best machine been a two seater. From the Fokker to the Spad in WWI to the Lightning and the Mustang in WWII to the F-86 in Korea they all carried one guy. People who had the strange predilection for this nonsense wanted the power of absolute control.

The Nam era came on the heels of an era of SAC dominance.

The 'bomber dominated' fifties were characterized by extremely tight controls on all flying operations They were, after all, carrying nuclear weapons.

They were also spending all the gold. The fighter forces were truncated and reduced to a fraction of SAC.

It was so unbalanced that by the late fifties, there were so few fighter slots out of pilot training that the Air Force had to do something. They guaranteed at least one fighter slot in each pilot training class. This was imperative, as many guys only went through the grind of training for a shot at fighters.

The competition was fierce, and often only the top guy got what he wanted.

Only even that wasn't true.

Because the only real fighters were the Tactical Air Command ones, the F-100's, the F-105's, and the F-4s. These were the full on "kill the enemy in the air and on the ground" machines.

The other fighters were in Air Defense Command. These guys sat alert, waiting to go get the Russian bombers that might try to take out Omaha.

Their flying was all air intercepts. Mostly high altitude stuff, it wasn't the real thing, or at least not to the real fighter jocks of TAC. Certainly, not to me.

The paucity of real fighters and the quality of the top graduates who got them led to an interesting phenomenon.

When the Nam air battle really exploded the first squadrons of fighters were loaded with cream, the major dudes.

In fact, many of the long term POW's in Hanoi were from this group. The fact they held up as well as they did is attributable to their elite make-up.

By the fall of '66 most of the originals had finished, one way or the other. Meanwhile the F-4's were rocking off the production lines. Replacements were needed, and lots of them. They pulled all of the fighter jocks that were out in the cold, say at some squirrely headquarters gig, and jammed them through F-4 school. And with them came many a brave triple "A" level player.

And headquarters knew that ultimately even the retreads wouldn't be enough so they convinced Congress to put a stick in the backseat of the F-4 and jam a pilot in there. I figure they knew it was bullshit but it gave them a bigger pool of meat with which to fight a protracted aerial battle. And it worked for everyone except the backseats who were trained to fly.

Don't get me wrong, a good navigator backseat was completely valuable.

The Navy knew that. They designed the F-4 to work with one pilot; it was the Air Force that screwed it up. We, the backseat pilots, were fucked and the good ones knew it.

One night I flew with some new guy who wasn't bad or good, just average. On the way home, leveled off and trimmed out, he says,

"You want to fly it, Oliver?"

"Fuck no, Captain."

"What do you mean, Lieutenant, are you kidding?"

"What I mean sir, is that holding the damn stick straight and level ain't shit and I don't want to do it."

"You have a bad attitude, mister."

"Maybe it will make me harder to kill...sir."

I loved saying that. It was impossible for anyone to get too pissed, but it just had enough sarcasm to get me off.

I found out later the jerk had told Hank about my comments.

"That's no way to build a career, alienating your superiors. You're considered a strange case, Oliver."

"Why? Because I wouldn't grab the little bone he throws my way? I'll grab the damn stick if one of the fronts tries to kill me, but I ain't no freakin' autopilot. How's that gonna help me learn how to fly this thing?"

One night I was with a guy I liked, named Baggins, in the Mugia Pass. Mugia was on the border of North Vietnam and Laos. It was a major transshipment point, beaucoup trucks and tres beaucoup guns.

Baggins rolls inverted and comes unplugged, unglued, completely vertigoed.

The beast is falling inverted toward the guns, towards the trucks, towards our death.

Baggins cries,

"Take it, take it. I've…"

That was all he had to say. I took it, went on instruments, rolled it over so the moon was overhead and pulled us out of the dive. I trimmed it up and gave it back to him. The thing is I dug Baggins, a great cat who had won an Illinois State Wrestling Championship in high school. But unlike Pappy Boyington, who translated his wrestling skills into superb aerial maneuvers, Baggins had no business in the beast.

Fighter flying is different and, really, each move is ephemeral. It is quick, distinct, over. It is psychic power married with mental flexibility that mattered; to be good took kind of an un-buyable non-thought.

CHAPTER 3

Buzz's Song

My frontseater for the first ten missions wasn't the guy I trained with at McDill, Hank Westerly, but a guy named Buzz Gann, who coincidently, had a buzz cut and who not coincidently, had gotten a Mig in the early summer of '67, some two months before my arrival.

The thing was, new backseaters had to fly with old frontseaters to get experience.

When I got there Buzz had ninety missions north, and flying the last ten with him proved to be an ordeal for both of us.

Why?

He was a wreck. He had that common combat thing-the "I know I'm going to get it on the last leg of the tour" syndrome.

He was a dislikable, irascible, self-involved prick, really.

But he was bright and totally cynical. I asked him once what getting the Mig was like and he said,

"The Mig 21 has a lot of design limitations."

End of conversation.

Thanks for the story, butthole.

This foretold the bizarre attitude in the Air Force about sharing important flying stories and ideas, especially dogfighting insights. Anyway we would climb in the cockpits and he would immediately start correcting me about a lot of trivial bullshit. I hadn't started the inertial quick enough, or hadn't figured the gross weight and other crap I found out later nobody else gave a shit about. At that point in my warrior development this was stinging.

I vowed to do better, but after riding with him I realized he cared and worried so greatly for his survival that he was unapproachable on a human level. He was crying out in muted anguish, really. It is possible he was actually deeply pained by the whole damn thing; but I never got to know him that well.

An interesting sidebar with him is we ran into one another in a fighter pilot bar at Homestead Air Force Base, near Miami, three years later when I was an old head frontseater.

"Hey Maj Buzz, how you doing? Remember me?"

He looks up from his drink, smiles slightly.

"Yeah, sure Oliver. You know I'd like to apologize for my behavior over there. I was a mess towards the end."

This was the first thing that came out of Buzz's mouth. It seems guys will do that sometimes if something is sticking in their conscience.

"That's okay. I found out later how you felt."

That was actually a lie. As in any male society, but perhaps to a greater degree this one, much was left unsaid. Actually, what I should have said,

"Yeah you were a real butt, Buzz, it was inexcusable. But, fuck, let's get drunk. Because we're both here, dammit, we're both still alive."

Later in my flight career, a flight happened that illustrates the principle of non- communication, even if death almost arrives.

I, with my backseater of course, was number Two flying a normal wing landing. We were on the right wing strictly watching our Lead. In other words: the technique is to stay right with the

Lead, not even to look at runway, just his wing tip. At maybe one hundred feet, Lead literally, it felt, snapped his plane back into me. I had to go full right rudder and almost full right stick to keep from hitting him. It was very close, very close. He had screwed up his runway alignment and was correcting way too fast. It was lousy flying and the worst part is if I hit the ground, my backseater and I would have died, and he would have survived. When we got on the bus there were several other crews there. I immediately went after this clown.

"You almost killed us. I had to use full fucking controls at less than one hundred feet. What the hell happened?"

There was nothing.

The bastard wouldn't even look at me. No response.

"Hey, I want an answer damn it. Maybe you didn't hear me. We almost hit the fucking ground on your wing, and it's generally considered a good idea not to do that. In fact I seem to remember being specifically told to never do that and since I had to fly through whatever the hell you were doing…"

At this point the dickhead finally looks at me and it dawns on him that he is a Major and he outranks me, though I don't really give a shit.

"Alright captain, that's enough."

There is a huge silence. Everyone is looking at me. I am looking at him. I knew I would never get on that guy's wing again. Never. I felt that I was fighting for the next poor slob that had to fly off this jerk.

I turned and walked back to the rear of bus muttering,

"Save your neck or save your brother, looks like it's one or the other."

Somebody laughed at my quoting The Band, but it had a hollow ring to it. By that time, after the war, I was hypersensitive to stupid flying.

Back to the Buzz man and our first bombing mission to the north.

The intelligence officer gave us the briefing and the prescribed target. The target was headquarters' idea of how we should be used.

"Of course, we think this target may be unproductive. This is what we would like to try if the first one's a dud."

He points to a spot on the map. It is on the mouth of the Dong Hoi River, just a few dots representing buildings. The Dong Hoi is the first major waterway north of the DMZ, running basically east to west. It would prove to be a recurring point of entry into the mysteries of the north.

"The guys targeting in Saigon rarely get anything right. We just freelance. You'll see."

Buzz is loquacious as usual.

I saw all right.

Buzz was leading. He puts Two into the usual extended trail position, about three miles back. As we approached the coast he pushed the power way up. Maybe 550 knots or so. It was hard to see much except the jungle, water and the occasional narrow road.

The headquarters target was an abandoned village, which Buzz is completely disinterested in. He takes us over to the alternative, the Da Nang derived target: the aforementioned buildings on the edge of the river. So far there has been no sign of ground fire. It's like a training mission. We orbit until Buzz says quietly,

"Lead is in with the bombs. Two, follow when you're ready."

My first pass in the North, and my hands are hanging worthlessly onto a hold below the canopy; all I could do is call off altitudes and hope Buzz does it well enough to get us through. It was not until much later that I thought about the first bombing run in terms of my own responsibility. Even then, of course, and even now, my ambivalence is palpable. Not damn sure what the warrior subgods will have to pay. It is like an extra burden, a heavy load in the karmic backpack that hangs there. I'd like to take it off someday and rest. But who knows?

Buzz pickles the load right on the altitude and really racks the thing up and out, as if climbing fast will help diminish the deed.

Suddenly Two is on the horn.

"Man, look at that."

We roll over and there is a huge fireball, then another one, and then more secondaries. The bombs had hit something big. I am suddenly thrilled, thinking it is amazing that the whole north side of the river is burning. All potential cosmic, ethical questions have to be put on hold, for my 23 year old brain is aflame with the age-old thrill of combat that is going my side's way.

"Jesus, look at that. Great shot, Captain."

"Not really."

Oh, I guess it's cool to be blasé.

The guy Buzz is so immune to effects that nothing but going home will impress him.

Buzz then calls Two into a rejoin and heads for home. In awhile he comes on the intercom, for what turns out to be a rare chat.

"If you must…celebrate a little. But don't get the idea that's normal. Most of the time our explosions are unanswered."

Normal! This guy is talking to me about normal? Yeah pal, this is normal. Flying this astounding machine up to some beautifully strange culture that has made different political decisions than us and then probably because of those decisions: BOMB THE HELL OUT OF THEM!!!

Back in the squadron I run off to tell the intelligence officer that he hit one. Yeah, I am fucking running on many simultaneous contradictory levels. I am scared, outraged, blood-lusted, amused, exhilarated, I'm certainly not exonerated, I may be doomed, and soon I will be drunk.

Suddenly it dawns on me. This guy, about 23 like me, was in another weird-ass position.

Two years earlier he was walking around South Bend wondering if the Irish would beat USC and if he was going all the way with Mary Joe. And now he was directing huge, almost unprecedented conventional bombing destruction. Gee, only an empire in full bloom could give a kid power like that.

CHAPTER 4

After Buzz, Back to Westerly

The compound where we were kept consisted of not only the air-conditioned reinforced barracks where Steve and I were during the rocket attack; it also had a theater, mess hall (though most pilots ate at the officers club) and even a racquetball court.

We even had our own Vietnamese maids, who beautifully sat on their haunches, doing laundry, chatting and laughing. It was a strange counterpoint to the dominant male culture. Sometimes I would crouch down next to them and try to feel the people we were intruding upon, trying to get something from them, something they couldn't give.

Outside, you could almost pretend you were in the States, if you just looked at the streets. But if you looked up, the sky was pulsating from explosions and incredible air traffic 24 hours a day including night air shows of prop gun ships spraying fire around the perimeter of the base. Sounds of choppers whomping and sirens wailing accompanied me as I took my daily constitutional. Always feeling that if I could just get back to Hank in one piece I had a better chance.

I get through ten North with Buzz and I'm heading back to the guy I trained with, the guy I trust, the guy who can get me through.

Hank calls me into a room at the squadron and delivers the bad news.

"They're making me the squadron maintenance officer."

"What's that mean?"

"That I won't be flying as much, this isn't peace time. Maintenance issues are amazing. Lots of planes getting hit, lots of 8 g loads that break stuff…"

"Uh, Major, who will I fly with? Do I get another frontseater?"

"No, you are going to be the roving backseater half the time. The other half of the flights you and I can go. Otherwise, you will fly with everybody, I guess. Especially the guys from wing and other part timers who don't have a regular backseater."

"That's fucked."

"I know."

I left Hank as soon as possible and headed to the squadron scheduling officer who is a captain named Faust.

"Uh, Captain Faust, this tour looks like we all made a pact with the devil, huh?"

Faust just looks at me.

I continue.

"I mean I just found out my frontseater Hank Westerly won't be able to fly with me a lot because they made him the maintenance officer, and I was wondering…"

Faust interrupts,

"You'll get your other missions with headquarters personnel and pilots whose backseaters are unavailable. I need a backseater like you around."

"These headquarters guys don't fly a lot, right?"

"So?"

"I was wondering about their proficiency, you know?"

"Most of them are senior officers, highly experienced."

Highly experienced in what, I wonder. I'm thinking so are a lot of minor leaguers, but there's a reason they never get to the bigs.

I can't yet find an angle to deal with the Faust, but I can hopefully find Kromer at the bar.

And there he is, Joe Kromer, another backseater that has 50 North, drinking because he had the day off.

I tell him what is happening with me and Hank.

"Man, you've been dicked. You won't know who the hell you are flying with. Sorry, Pal."

Kromer knew that flying skills varied greatly, and hence, survival rates varied greatly depending on who you were with.

Kromer looks at my martini and says,

"Well, your tour just became a lot like that drink; it's got a twist in it."

CHAPTER 5

Maids Mourn

When I get back to the barracks, the Vietnamese maids are crying. Sitting in a circle, rocking on their heels and crying.

I pause beside them, confused, when Steve Montague walks up.

"Did you hear we lost Hughes and Bobby?"

I hadn't, I was befuddled and a little drunk.

I looked questioningly at Steve, and looked at the maids and Steve said.

"They loved Bobby. He spent time with them, kidded them."

I say,

"So much for the Asian indifference to death theory so popular with some guys around here."

Steve nodded and I head for my room, pissed and sad.

CHAPTER 6

Crash to the Right

It came to pass soon enough that Hank is fixing broken Phantoms, so I draw some cat named Hopple, a nice enough schnook who should have been flying cargos or something.

We brief, then go through fence down the walkway past refugees with all possessions, through the Vietnamese Rangers throwing knives at each others feet, past the airlines disgorging new recruits, the stewardess standing looking down at us. I'm looking up at them shy, craving, (hell I'm jacking off two times a night) but the mission adrenaline is overpowering, past the South Vietnamese choppers, past the big props, who are the sprayers, the forest killers, and finally to the hulks, big and quiet.

Flights went off every 45 minutes round the clock; right now our squadron had night flights. I have that queasy feeling as I walk out on the line with Hopple when a Phantom suddenly lights the burners. Muffled and crackling both - the sound and the flame lashing rearward-I give a silent beseechment the crew is and will be all right. Bouncing, accelerating, the plane wobbling from one tiny piece of rubber to the other, the thing doesn't so much fly as it power-staggers into the Vietnamese blackness. It was cooler at night, refreshing almost, as I tried to grasp what the hell it could mean. Like a kid in the air show it held me in awe until I realized that I would be doing the same thing in 45 minutes.

Take off has a sense of unreality, especially at night.

"But once the plane had taken off, the night once more grew full of beauty and enthrallment; for now the womb of night was carrying life."

St. Exupery had that right, though we were carrying the antithesis of life.

We were number Two on a radar bombing ride that goes smoothly, the destruction mere flashes under the thick weather.

The Lead tells Hopple to stay in trail for recovery at Da Nang.

As we get close, approach control informs us the ceiling is 500 feet and the visibility is one mile. Here's a note on weather flying. The brilliant powers that be had neglected to provide the plane with an ILS, a system that allows an aircraft to fly a very precise, crosshatched final approach. The pilot kept two bars, one horizontal and one vertical, centered. This led him to a spot on the runway at a decent angle. A key thing about the system was it didn't require ground control radar guys yakking at a stressed out pilot. But when the Air Force bought the F-4 it was a navy design, and the damn navy didn't believe in the ILS because it can't be used in a carrier landing. So we had to be talked down by some guy in a shack somewhere.

Someone told me later that they could have outfitted the entire fleet of fighters for a few million.

Well, the taxpayers were about to pay almost that much for the stunt the Hopple was going to perform. I looked down a mile out on the final; there was a strange inconsistency to the visibility. I could see the lights on the ground, then we would go into thick clouds, and back out again.

Weird weather. Buffeting winds and impossible rain.

The GCA guy was working hard to keep Hopple on the glide path.

"Turn right to 010. You're 20 feet high on the glide path. Turn right to 020. Red Two, you are way left of the center line."

The GCA guy kept trying to get us back on runway alignment.

I remember thinking how suddenly black it was.

Deep black.

But we were being blown hard to the left, by a nasty ass right cross wind. The sounds of a fully engaged, overmatched operator of the beast came through my headphones. Hopple was worried. He couldn't get on top of the situation.

He was 'behind.'

If you let your control of the monster get 'behind'...it could eat you alive, spit you out of the burner cans. Hopple had opened the cage and I was the unfortunate assistant zookeeper along for the chase.

When we broke out at 500 feet I thought maybe, just maybe, the monster might still be controllable.

I could see the runway to the right. I could not only see the water on the canopy, I could also feel the rain. Somehow the two primal forces, wind and rain, howling, shredding, tore at our delicate balance and ripped the rest of the cage door off.

Only we didn't know it yet.

Hopple tried. He corrected back to the right and banged the thing on the runway. Then he did the coup de grâce to our chances.

He popped the drag chute!

Immediately the direction of the plane turns right.

Why?

Because we weather vaned into the wind, helped by the chute and the hydroplaning of the wheels. We were essentially sailing across the runway, at a forty-five degree angle.

Hopple cried,

"I CAN'T HOLD IT. I CAN'T HOLD IT!!!"

He had left full rudder, left nose wheel steering, left aileron and still the direction was hard right to the edge of the runway.

I screamed.

"Right throttle, RIGHT THROTTLE!!!"

Hopple responds to my pleading. He jams the right engine all the way to the afterburner. This might have worked if he had done it earlier. Because of the differential nature of the thrust, the right engine at full power pushes the fuselage to the left.

But it was too damn late. All the extra thrust did was give us more speed as we hit the edge of the concrete.

The beast leapt out of its cage!

We were in uncharted jungle here, but I couldn't run. Strapped onto a metal seat, all I could do was prepare to die. For I was convinced we had no chance. These fuckers were dangerous normally, and this was highly abnormal.

NOISE…TEARING>>>HORRIBLY   BLINDINGLY TENTANACIOUSLY LOUD NOISE>

All I could hear was the fucker coming apart and it was screaming itself to death.

I'm going to die.

I'm going to die.

I'm going to die.

That's all I could say to myself, all I could comprehend.

Most death scenes are eventually kind of quiet, or at least that's what I maybe think, but here it was loud, baby, loud.

The beast is on its own, fighting and bouncing through the grass but…looming in the grass ahead lies another enemy of escaped 130-knot monsters.

The marines had installed a cable arresting system, consisting of two concrete block houses, one on either side of the runway. Between, laid flat across the runway, was a big fat aircraft carrier cable. Inside the block houses were two huge drums to wind up and release the cable. Purpose? To stop the F-4 and other fighters who had the ability to catch the cable with their hooks.

In front of this concrete block was a trench. In front of the trench stood a solitary marine with a gun and a grim expression, water dripping off his helmet. His job is to protect this concrete block from all enemies. Suddenly he hears something different, different from the rain, different from the wind, different from even the captured beasts that roll out screaming over there to his right on the runway. The sound comes from straight ahead…he looks into the dark…when it appears: the electric eyeball that used to be a landing light coming right at him.

If he wasn't right next to the trench, he doesn't make it.

But he was!

And he did the one thing that prevented the monster from devouring him. He dove onto the trench.

I've often wondered if we could have ridden the thing to a slow resolution of its rage. I doubt it. It seems to me that it would have hit a depression or a little rise; tilted over and burned itself and us up in rainy agony.

No one would have heard our screams.

But life and plane crashes turn on the strangest chances. This particular piece of concrete block was three feet or so off the ground. The bottom of the beast's wings was three feet off the ground, so it was a perfect match. The concrete relieved the beast of everything under the wings and under the nose too.

All that was landing gear ripped off. All that was tip tanks sheared off. All that was bomb racks…gone.

But now, though it's been relieved of its ability to gallop, it finds itself momentarily able to fly again. We soared into the night for a glorious moment. It got quiet suddenly and then… for the last time…the monster settled rather gently in a grassy, watery grave. Only…

It refused to take its incompetent handler and his terrified assistant with it into death. In its wake lay a stunned marine in a trench with three former landing gears strewn about him, the wheels of one leg still turning. The beast became a paraplegic; not much different from many of its former human allies who also left bloody parts in watery trenches.

I am still alive and an electric thought shoots through me.
GET OUT!

But there was no way. I was completely ensnared in all the gear…gear to hold us in our seat; gear to hold the chute straps; gear to pull our legs out during an ejection.

Fuck!!

Why can't I get out? When I tried to stand up and I mean…I…wrenched…myself upward…full of the adrenaline of new hope.

There was this massive CONSTRAINT!!!

I looked down. And the act of seeing, dimly, the belt around me awoke in my psyche the realization again of who the hell I was and what had just happened. Emergency release handle will cut all this shit loose. I pull it and it cuts all the constraints; I try to stand up again and I hit my helmet hard on the canopy.

The canopy!!!

I grope for the switch, crouched on the seat. There it is. I pull it and…nothing. It won't open. What the hell? Something… maybe there's no pneumatic pressure. I pull the emergency 'blow the canopy switch.' It's gone with a whoosh. Amazingly, water was suddenly everywhere, then a huge thump just to my left. I fear the beast is still ready to blow. Jump to the right wing…get ready for the three feet jump to the ground, but its right there.

THERE'S NO GEAR!!

It's a short step to the ground. I really didn't know or grasp that we had lost everything under the wings.

Run, Run, Run.

Through the rain I was slipping on the lush grass scrambling away from the monster. It must have anger and rage left. I slow then, stop and turn to look. I can dimly see it in the distance, a low dark hulk, bathed off and on by red flashing lights from the tower. The beast had, at those strange terror and thrill filled moments stolen my soul and put it inside its fuselage and sunk its fuel stained fangs deep in me.

I suddenly loved the beast, at that moment, in the middle of the stinking exciting war, I fell in love. And when I later went to the frontseat and when I got very, very, good…I could see that was when it had hooked me. Right at that crazy assed moment when Hopple had wounded it and it still had enough love for its creators not to kill us back.

Then Hopple shows up.

While in drenched, silent contemplation of my love object, Hopple fucking appears. Just steps out of wet darkness and looks at me. And when he does I go into a scream. I wrench my helmet off and slam it to the ground.

"That was completely fucked!! You should never have pulled the drag chute; you should have pushed the right engine quicker. All you did, Hopple, was keep our fucking speed up so we could leave the runway with about 130 damn knots…"

Now Hopple is running around me trying to get me to calm down. Scurrying to and fro saying,

"Now Oliver it's alright, it's alright."

It dawns on me through my rant that this guy's worried about my testimony as to his incompetence. The Air Force takes seriously people breaking their equipment. Especially since fucking Le May and the bomber jerks had gotten control of the balls of the service in the '50s and early '60s. Careers have been lost over flying accidents. This careerist puke almost kills us and then doesn't even let his real emotions show, just tries to calm me down.

But I'm not done.

"Man, Hopple, you sure fucking got out fast. I had to blow my canopy because there was no pressure left."

Hopple looks at me, and smiles a bit.

"It almost hit you. It came down right next to you."

I realize then the noise after I blew the canopy was the thing going up and crashing straight down. Only the huge wind pushing it slightly to the side prevented its 300 pounds from landing on me.

Hopple keeps smiling.

"I was wondering if you would ever get out."

Wild-eyed I looked at him.

"I've been chasing you for awhile. You're pretty fast for a fat boy."

I know what Hopple's trying to do. He's trying to use psychology to calm me down.

"You didn't fly fighters before this did you, Hopple?"

I almost feel guilty as he turns away, but we both know at that moment that he has failed the test.

He doesn't belong.

He continues to beseech me as the Jeep drives us to the squadron. Before I was in awe of the beast, a little scared of it. Now I'm hopelessly in love, I can't believe how compelling it looks, and I can't believe what it was sent through and how it kept us alive. All I can do is look over my shoulder at my new obsession hunkering gearless in the monsoon-soaked weeds.

CHAPTER 7

Crash to the Right Hangover

Rolling over in my bed after the post crash party, still half drunk, my flight suit lying like the Phantom monster out there in the grass, crumpled and damp.

Through the headache, I can hear myself saying there's no way out; no way to pretend I can leave this dance as a bridesmaid, there's no way I can fly anything else if I survive 80 more counters.

Here's the problem.

The rule goes like this: if a backseater wishes to go to the front, to move six lateral feet forward he must volunteer to come back to the circular three dimensional nightmare space of the Nam.

Another tour, another one hundred North and God knows how many elsewhere. It's professional blackmail; it's diabolical; it's logical empire thinking.

Who better to handle the thing than someone who's had to watch others handle the thing. What hellishly amazing and priceless training.

The moral considerations are impossible. The contradictions palpable. I know the war's fucked.

I know we're going to lose.

I know I'm compromising my soul, but I can't stop myself.

Maybe Kromer can talk me out of it.

"Well, in the first place, Oliver, you might not make it through this one so…" He shrugs, takes a drink, and looks at me as if he knows gallows humor ain't the issue.

"Could you stand yourself if you don't upgrade and come back?" He asks.

"No." I say.

And I can't stand myself if I do.

Kromer elucidates further.

"Listen, man, it's an issue with all the juicy deals: moral courage, physical courage, professional pride, compromise, death, and love."

"Love?"

"Yeah. Which do you love the most? Your youthful obsessions or your lifelong consciousness?"

"I have to experience it. The frontseat. I have to. It ain't love… it's lust."

As often happens, we're collecting eavesdroppers and because I am a loud motherfucker when I get excited, I get a little embarrassed by my fervor so I do the male thing, stop talking about it and change the subject.

Besides, the subject is closed. I'm volunteering to come back.

And therefore finishing this tour is now more than ever all about speed and survival. I resolve to do anything to get through fast, and the hell with any rules but my own.

And the only way to get out early and alive was to get 100 missions in North Vietnam faster than anyone else.

If I had to pull tricks, I'd pull tricks.

If I had to bend rules, I'd bend rules.

I knew if I came back, my experience would give me power, and I was going to use that to cut losses, stupid, awful, mindless losses.

I think back to childhood, to the Korean War, when my Dad was a maintenance officer, taking care of F-80s and F-86s.

I was a hero-worshipping 10 year old, loving the fighter pilots my old man was succoring.

They must be great, to actually do that, to fly the fastest machines on earth. They must be the best, I thought.

I had missed my Dad, and this was my compensation, to know that he was helping the coolest guys on the planet.

Now, still drunk and internally shaken I more and more realized a lot of the fronts really suck and I've got to get out quick or die.

CHAPTER 8

River Mines

I get Hank back for a night flight.

The problem with night flying in the north was what to do. There were no FACs. It was black, baby. Targets weren't rare, they were just impossible to see.

One day the bird brains who sat somewhere in Saigon deciding how we would risk our asses in the dark came up with a beauty.

We were directed to drop a new horror on the north.

River mines.

Here was the deal. If we could get low enough, say 50 feet off the water, we could deliver magnetically triggered water mines into the murky depths of the rivers. Here they would sink to the bottom and wait. Wait for what? Why, hey, they would wait for an unsuspecting boat to come a-floating down.

The deep thinkers in Saigon can see it in their dreams. The Chairman Ho departs Dong Hoi at sunset. It's a scow loaded with munitions (what else?) that's moving west to rendezvous with human mules north of the DMZ. Everything looks fine. It's a milk run with the thick cloud cover and the rice cooking and one of the guys catches some fish…

Suddenly they encounter the perfect American technology: we can make money and kill terrorists in one perfect moment…. BIG BANG!

These mine things have a metal sensor that can detect the boat's metal hull and then fire themselves off.

No more Chairman Ho, or at least his floating namesake.

Cool deep thinking, that.

I was on the first mission with this new marvel. It's another potential nightmare; this time in blackness.

Hank Westerly was interested in this sucker a bunch. He knew it would be a feather in his helmet if he led this thing well.

The only feather I wanted was another counter.

Counters!

It took one hundred rides above the DMZ, into the North, to get a ride home.

More on that later.

Westerly is on my ass during planning.

"Oliver, I want some real planning on this one. Work on it with the other backseater and get it right."

But we both knew it was a bitch to try to do this to split second timing. Because here's the rub. Westerly wants us to come down the river in one direction towards the target, while the other 'bird' or number Two comes heading the other way. We arrive about twenty seconds ahead of Two, so we can lay down some nasty ass cbu's to suppress the flak. And while the poor fucks are dodging or dying from that brilliant invention, Two can waltz in and lay upon the waters the second benediction - twelve 750 pound river mined babies.

Neat huh?

"Look, Major Westerly, this could be impossible." I say, "To get the timing perfect, at night with no check point, I can't really verify once we've separated from Two…"

"Use the inertial navigation. You're the backseater-navigator."

The bastard was intentionally calling me a navigator, instead of a pilot. He wasn't real crazy about me anyway, partially because I'm about 25 pounds overweight, and I'm loud, profane and disrespectful. He wants academy men to project the lean, mean…etc. Westerly is West Point '55 and I am United States Air Force Academy '65. I'll give him that distinction-he's tall and lean like all great ones are supposed to be. Actually, I'd trained with him in the States and he could fly. He'd been through F-86's and F-100's, a real 50s trained jock who finally got his chance to fight. Big thing for guys like him.

I say, "sure Major I'm going to navigate my ass off, right after I get myself a couple sandwiches and a coke."

Westerly gives me the mildly disgusted look.

Do I care?

We're losing planes right and left. Every mission there are amazing explosions. We're fucking sub-gods… and gods can be any size they want, Westerly, do you understand? Hell, I go on enough of these fuckin' missions and I may not fit through the damn door. There's real power here and you're worried about waistlines.

Jesus.

Am I the only one who comprehends what's going on here?

After Westerly left, Sam Webber, the number Two backseater, and I started planning. We worked our butts on the problem. How to time it perfectly, so that the flak suppression is still exploding when Two lays the bombs out? Two can't jink or dodge while they are dropping. He's vulnerable as hell for those 15 seconds.

Here's another thing. In World War II, the allies decided to take out a dam in Nazi Germany. So the B-25 crews trained their asses off to get the bombing right. They trained hard for weird shit like that. We are about to fly equally weird shit extemporaneously, at high speeds, and in pitch black. No practice, no training, just another crazy ass ride.

Here's what we finally decide to do.

Taking off separately at a 30 second interval, Two rejoined us and we headed north, but not towards the target area. We went to an island off the coast of North Vietnam. The moon outlined the western side of supposedly uninhabited rock as we leveled our wings and zeroed our inertial navigators.

"Three, two, one, set."

My voice sounds quiet and a little slow.

Then we split up.

Splitting two ships at night was very unusual. If there was a problem, you had no back up, and no way to know where the plane and the pilots went down. Damn, these bombs must be really important.

Two goes towards the northeast and the mouth of the unsuspecting river; ol' Hank and I go due west toward another spot on the same, hopefully sleeping waterway.

If the timing worked we would hit an exact point on the river at the precise time Two hits the mouth of the Dong Hoi. From then on it was a matter of holding speed and staying on the river as we steamed towards each other.

Maybe.

I look up and think of the old fighter pilot axiom-always schedule night flying on a full moon. For a change they got it right. I could almost read my map by it. But was it a map worth reading? We are flying distance and heading with no confirmation over pitch-black jungle trying to hit a particular twist on the river.

Suddenly Hank pushed us down roller coaster style.

"I got the river. Two, we're approaching base leg, turning to heading 020."

"Roger Lead. Two heading 200…on time."

Hank takes us down, I mean down. Right on the freaking water. I'm thinking maybe if he goes any lower the submersion will count as a baptism.

A couple of sadly late tracers sling themselves behind us. We're too fast for that weak shit.

"How's our timing. Oliver?"

"I think…ask Two for position. Should be thirty seconds."

Here's where it gets sticky. Westerly calls Two.

"Two, what's your time to target?"

There's no answer for about twenty seconds, which can be very long indeed. Then.

"Two is through the run, Lead. We're pulling out of here."

You could hear the g's coming though the radio. The guy was using all the energy he had to egress. He then said the magic words…though they had a sarcastic edge to them.

"There's heavy ground fire. Serious tracers. Two's heading home….Lead."

I can tell the cat ain't happy we didn't make it ahead of him, and his tone tells me so.

So fucking what?

He made it without us. Only one problem I notice though, is Hank's not pulling up. We're still down on the river.

"You dicked the timing, Oliver."

He jams the throttles into burner.

"Yeah, well we don't need to flak suppress now, major. Let's get out of here. We can talk about it at home."

But Hank don't pull up.

Hank keeps us down there, down in the teeth of the aroused, down in the river valley of maybe our needless death, we stoke on.

I do have a few problems with my philosophy, you see. I know we're subgods. Of course. How else could we have such power at our fingertips? But I also know we can die and seem to be doing so at an alarming rate. Further this destruction comes sometimes from those little peons below. Now…risking this death against the unsuspecting people at 4,500 feet seems a fair nah-nah-nah-nah-nah-nah. But we ain't at 4,500, we ain't a single hundred.

We're 45 feet period. Maybe less. But here's the real conundrum. We have a choice. We can fucking leave. This is what makes our game different from the guns waiting for us. They can't depart and be grilling a steak and drinking whiskey in half an hour. We just pull this little stick between our legs, twist it to the right and are GONE-MAN-GONE. And nobody will care.

For isn't that the difference between man and the other animals? The ability to choose. And what is the difference between man and the gods? That's the ability to choose wisely, to go beyond codes and to go beyond face.

But Hank can't see this. He sees loss of face. I can see loss of all other parts of the body.

I say as calmly as possible,

"Two says the gunners have been alerted. Perhaps even irritated. Perhaps even really fucking mad. There is no point in laying down suppression for someone who's half the way back to Da Nang."

No answer.

Camus once said that the higher animals have a right to their moods and right now ol' Hank is a mad ass mammal.

Before I can try again to reason with the fucker, the cockpit illuminates, and light is pouring in from above. What the...?

It looked like a lattice of light, like an X of light centering over the plane. Guns on both sides of the river have brought their shots down as low as they can without hitting each other and it's not quite low enough to get us. Swords made of tracers saluting the marriage of centuries old warfare and new technology in the middle of a steamy jungle.

It reminded me somehow of the crossed swords that brides and grooms go through at the academy. You know, that corny shit at the end of the guy's senior year where they marry some high school sweetheart after four years of cloisterhood.

"Don't pull up! Don't pull up!"

I'm screaming at Westerly, although this time he can't fail to see what's happening. Often the back can see flak better than the front. The front ejection seat blocks the backseaters view forward, but to the rear the canopy affords the poor bastard riding aft a superior viewing angle of fire coming from the sides and back. I spent much of the time yelling instructions to the front during attack and most of them obeyed. If they didn't I refused to fly with them. More on that later, too.

Then, suddenly the deadly lights are gone. I look up at distant illumination. The stars may be indifferent to our existence, but the moon beams silently at us through tropic air, and I'm grateful to see any light that isn't trying to kill me.

Black. Just sweet black night.

It had come back as quickly as it had left.

It was over.

Hank pulls up with surprising gentleness, rolls to the right and we both looked down to the darkness, trying to see that which couldn't be seen.

"I never dropped the damn things. It was too hairy to move to the shore to get anything off. But that doesn't mean you're off the hook, Oliver. What happened to the timing?"

"Excuse me if I'm not ready for debriefing right now....sir."

You could say sir many ways. This 'sir' had anger, disgust, and abated fear.

Fuck him. We both just missed dying and he's pissed that a complex navigation problem didn't go right the first time through.

This clown in the front had just tried his almost best to help the North Vietnamese kill us while pretending to want to kill them-the dumbest fucking dance I've seen since the last USO show. Then he has the temerity to be upset about some totally meaningless timing glitch. I've got to survive the bullets from the other team and the macho bullshit from my own.

The contradiction on the bloody ground fighting between glory and death is well documented, but in the air there can apparently still be a naïve idea of obligation based on face.

"On the fields of friendly strife are sown the seeds that on other fields and other days will bear the fruits of victory."

MacArthur said that.

"On the fields of freaking war the horseshit rules and honor of friendly strife don't mean a fucking thing."

Oliver said that.

Both Hank and General Douglas MacArthur were laced with West Point's poisonous conditioning; every game counts. Right?

But the guys like us that fought aren't the real gamesters. The real gamesters are the guys that can sell the idea of war.

The squadron dropped these absurdities for a week up and down the Dong Hoi River. On the last night the plane with the bombs was, presumably, hit. No one knows for sure but they didn't report for late night drinking as usual. They were just gone.

The powers suspended the missions until two days later when a report came from headquarters. Seems a long range reconnaissance patrol had seen an interesting sight. A crowd of North Vietnamese was on the shores of the river in a festive mood, looking up river and laughing. Around the bend came several floating 50 gallon drums, appropriately painted red. As the drums approached the spectators there was an under water explosion, refreshing the folks with a nice shower and sending the drums 30 feet in the air.

CHAPTER 9

Seventy-Two Big Ones

A steamy fall tropical day. It's a good day to be at the beach which I never went to but instead I'm listening to a briefer who says we're to contact a FAC who is off the Pac One coast. He supposedly has a special target.

"Oh, by the way, you will be carrying an unusual load, eighteen 750 pound bombs."

I sat upright from my usual slouch.

"What?"

Even Hank was impressed.

Looking incredulous, I ask him.

"Can we do that?"

"Look it up."

I do and we can, even though it's over 13,000 pounds of death and mayhem. It's way more than the biggest WWII bombers could do. It befits us. Now more than ever I'm convinced we are the chosen ones.

Fuck, after this flight I'm optimistic the NVA might surrender immediately.

When we got to the flight line I stepped out of the van and almost gasped. The beast looked burdened. There were bombs everywhere. There were bombs in places I didn't know would carry bombs.

Westerly says, while we're pre-flighting the bird,

"What the hell are we going to do with all these bastards?"

He seems a bit worried. Not frightened, but precognitively aware that this ride is going to effect him in some new way. I mostly admired Westerly, though he had that taciturn nature of many of the best jocks and though he would occasionally utter the usual banal bullshit about this being the only war we had, so we should enjoy it. It was that kind of 1950s fighter pilot crap. And of course he tried to kill us on the river mine run.

But he knew or sensed more than that.

The take-off roll didn't have that usual initial jolt. When this amount of weight overcomes inertia, there is no huge immediate push when the afterburners clap on; just earnest, hard-won acceleration. The thing could do this, could carry this but it wouldn't be easy.

Banging back and forth between two surprisingly small tires, she reluctantly gets up to rotation speed. It's the equivalent of harnessing a powerful racehorse to a huge sled and making it pull and pull and pull.

Just yesterday, one of my Academy classmates had aborted a take-off run at Cam Ran Bay and rolled up on the end of the runway. Severe burns for him and death for the frontseater.

We break ground and Hank turns left over the bay. I can see the bleached boned look of the sand and little American toy soldiers speckled on the sea. This is always a strange part of the ride. I can look at the sky or ground or into the overrated radar, which we won't need today, but I can't look at the faces of the enemy, unless I happen to catch a news broadcast of McNamara.

We got to the DMZ, staying over the water, when the FAC came up on our frequency.

"Gunfighter, what have you got?"

"Four, with eighteen 750s each."

"Perfect, what I've got are the most persistent anti-aircraft batteries ever seen by man or dog."

Just another wise-ass FAC. They seem to think this nightmare deserves some kind of grade C comedy rap. This clown wants to kill anti-aircraft.

Shit.

Guns.

We rarely attack guns. It's trucks and ammo dumps we seek; guns are usually the last resort. Attacking anti-aircraft is self-defeating, that's what the North wants us to do. If we're fighting the guns we ain't stopping the trucks. That's the way I saw it, but this FAC had a hard on for these people down there and he wanted them dead. He was an assistant god and had that right, I guess. I'm still trying to digest his stupid idea, when he comes back on.

"I'm over water. No way to survive if I get over close to them. I'll try to fire a rocket towards them."

"No need, we can see their flak, and it looks like 37 millimeter."

Westerly isn't excited as he tells this to the FAC. It's weird because we're already at about thirteen thousand feet, for us that's way high. It's more than anything a kind of floating dream.

There's no danger; they can't hit us, and that's very weird.

"Gunfighter, loose right wing formation. We're going to 22,000, roll in for one pass, release all ordinance and return to base in trail. Pull out by ten thousand."

"Two."

"Three."

"Four."

We climb slowly, inexorably. I want those people to quit shooting. Their little explosions are increasingly small, almost pathetic, like cum marks on an old green sheet.

I can still see that day.

Clear blue sky.

The coast line with white-capped waves splashing into green, green jungle canopy. The Dong Hoi River is to the west, the island we used for the freaking mine mission just to the east. Neither Westerly nor I say anything. We just climb with this impossible load.

"Call out the altitudes, Oliver, I want to pickle at fifteen." That should get us out before eight thousand. The 37 millimeters got no chance to hit us."

"Yeah."

Westerly pulls the thing over, adding power to keep it stable, and then a sixty-degree dive. It looks straight down. In a steep dive, it always feels steeper from inside. Especially this one. I call off the altitudes, 23, 22, 21…"

Westerly moves to the left, then right.

18, 17, 16 and at 15 he starts the sequence. They come off alternatively left, right, left, right. Each bomb sending a tiny jolt through me. The whole thing seems like a long, long time. Finally we're empty, completing the debasement. And we start the 5 g pull out, turn left, and head south. I want so many freaking g's I'll black out, but consciousness stays.

Westerly normally would turn to have a look, but this time we just keep going.

The FAC comes on air and all he says is,

"Jesus, that's awesome!"

Seven minutes after the bombs hit we're on final approach at Da Nang. The whole damn thing took thirty minutes.

Majors and above live in trailers; air-conditioned Americana. I have never been in one, nor wanted the privilege. But Hank surprises me and says,

"Come on over to the trailer, I've got some good scotch."

I just nodded; we weren't drinking pals, but this…

With their little coffee nook, the orange red carpet and the linoleum covered table, they had it all in those trailers. All they needed was some nice pictures of mountain streams or maybe

Cleveland on the wall. But, it was war and you can't have everything.

We began serious drinking.

Westerly looks at his glass and starts talking.

"Who the hell are those guys? They didn't have a chance, not a fucking chance. I mean if they quit shooting we couldn't have seen them, they had to know that but they kept on…"

I asked him if he knew who Bernard Fall was. Westerly looked a little surprised,

"No."

"He was a French journalist who was here with the foreign legion. Actually the French fought well but they were spread out over North and South Vietnam and Laos. The VC really handed them their asses. They would ambush the legion and then the stragglers would spend weeks staggering back to French outposts. Fall asked the same questions. Who were these people and then he asked another question? Who were the French to try and keep them under colonial rule?"

Westerly wasn't looking at me, just staring into his medicine, when he says,

"I graduated from the Point while the French were here. Hell, it was sickening. I've spent ten years getting ready for combat and then to have to do that."

Hank looks at me and says something I'll never forget.

"I'd rather be on a mission where they had a chance."

Then he says,

"God, I love to fly."

Yes, yes they must have a chance, a chance to get you. Otherwise it's an execution, and neither of us signed up for that.

It's strange because the contradiction was most palpable at that moment, it summed up in a perfect way the ultimate dilemmas of the pure warrior faced with the reality of his profession…

I stayed with him a little longer until silence descended over us both…

I staggered out of the trailer; over my shoulder he's pouring another drink as I close the door. We'll both have to think about it some, alone.

But I'm not ready for that yet, so it's off to the bar.

My temple, my church, it's the only profane holiness I know.

When I walk in another guy from the flight is there. He seems real drunk and he's talking to a pilot I'd never seen before.

"Hey Oliver, this is the FAC: Stormy '66."

The FAC starts pumping my hand.

"That was incredible; man I'd never seen anything like it. My O-2 was bouncing all over the sky from the impacts. Those gunners had a very bad day."

"Yeah," I said.

"That'll teach 'em."

Squatting

Squatting in her caved out back

I tweaked the multiple tits

And out spits noise and light.

It wants to come like everything else

And boy does the semen flow from this girl.

She's all orifices and dicks and stuff.

Her hardness promises sanctuary but, really, it's all fluid and

Death with her.

CHAPTER 10

Biggest Asshole in the Squadron

He looked like Johnny Cash, if you can picture that cat with a flight suit and an aura of death. He reminded me of a demented southern preacher, if that's not a redundancy. He was the only guy I ever flew with or against that seemed genuinely evil. He hated me and I hated him from almost first sight. It was visceral and almost pleasurable, the enmity I had for him; I relished it and nurtured it. There was a mutual fire between us. He called me a jailhouse lawyer. His strut came from three Migs he got in Korea, and there was nothing like having destroyed another plane, the Super Bowl for fighter pilots. The variables in that dance, however, dictated caution. You just didn't know who the guy had killed and under what circumstances. I figured the North Koreans he got were some poor kids who could barely get the thing off the ground, which was the norm in that bloody encounter. It didn't matter; the prick's status was assured.

One day I'm driving Major Kuster, that's his name, and the other three guys in his flight out to their planes. The crews ride in bread vans with two facing bench seats, rather pedestrian compared to the open jeeps of World War II. Our flight suits were bags with zippers; our boots were the jungle ones just like the grunts, we had mesh vests with lots of stuff like radios, and batteries and a pistol and little food or water. Indeed, our birds were hot, but the rest of the look and the feel that sucked me into this game from post-toddler play on, wasn't here. And dammit, it somehow mattered. It's funny, I didn't care that we didn't sing fighting songs and slap each other on the back like those stupid RAF flicks but something wasn't right.

And pricks like Kuster were the worst. He's running his mouth and I'm seething on the fucker. I was starting to feel real good, hating his ass that much. Who wanted to be in sub-god level with him? I wanted him to get it in the skull and have the backseater bring the thing home.

A C-130...who I noticed on my left...without right of way...jams his engines and pulls out in front of me. I pull up from my slouch over the wheel...bang the brakes-HARD! I had to, in order to prevent hitting the dumb ass prop jock. Every one in the back goes on the floor...Kuster because he's in the front is on the bottom. There's gear and boots and flight suits swimming together. It was great watching him flop around until he finds his voice. I mean he really got in touch with his anger. He told me he was getting ready to go drop bombs on people that he hated less than he hated my ass. He really hurt me with that one. Sure major. Like I care about your fucking dignity especially since I saved you from being chopped into little bits by huge propellers.

"Wait until I get back."

Oh gee, was he going to do something bad to me? Like make me fly combat in the back of semi guided missiles with fucks like him.

Actually I'll have to give him credit. He did the one thing that really hurt. He put me on 'desk' for eighteen hours a day indefinitely.

The desk.

Command central for the squadron, it vibrated 18 to 20 hours a day. A normal shift was half that and it was exhausting-manning the phones, driving crews out and back, talking to maintenance, filing reports, checking weather and a bunch of other crap. If a plane didn't come back, it became hellish. People milling, wondering…a quiet funeral like tone. In normal times, I didn't hang around for that, I headed for the bar, but Kuster had crucified me to the desk.

Nice move, you bastard. You can see the worst thing, of course. I couldn't fly, and I couldn't get counters. No movement toward the bloody finish line. There was just the desk day after day.

When Kuster came by he would pause and look at me, waiting for the break, the lunge. If I swing at him, I'll be court-martialed, which is what he wants. The fuck had guts, I'll say that. But I didn't break; I had been up against other clowns at the blue zoo who could haze as an art form. Way better than his cracker ass, but then they were way smarter than his cracker ass.

The Air Force Academy understood modern mathematics training, but the Neanderthals from West Point who had gone into the Air Force jammed that archaic Hudson River, sadistic monk jive onto a first rate engineering school.

About the fifth day a cool major named Johnson, who outranked the prick, looked at me quizzically and said,

"What are you doing on the desk all the time, Lieutenant?"

"Major Kuster is punishing me for stopping too fast…sir. Maybe he wanted to be decapitated by a prop. An anachronistic end for such a distinguished jet jock but who am I…"

I looked up to see the Major half smiling and holding up his hand.

"I don't think I want to hear this. This is your last shift."

Three hours later I staggered into the bar. Buck Owens was hearing Little Rock calling, homesick tears were calling, Little Rock was calling him back home.

Pauly was a moonlighting sergeant behind the surprisingly nice wooden bar. Chosen for his discretion, he was about to be tested.

"The usual, Pauly."

When I turned around with my double scotch, the bacchanalian bomber boogie hadn't really started. The real drunkenness would wait for midnight or later This round-the-clock attack was great for alcoholics like my pals and me. Ah, the 3:00 am stories, the 3:45 am stories, new tales of death and destruction, kind of like TV. If you don't like the story of one mission just drink and wait for the next one. Most everyone came in to drink except the Mormons - there seemed to be a lot of those geeks in this honored and bloody cult. But then who wanted to drink with second rate Christians anyway? I mean Jesus stopping by North America on his way home. Come on. If I was him I would have gone to Havana.

Oh my…shit, I can't believe it. Fucking Kuster is at the table with the only real dish of a nurse on the whole base. Why did she pick that prick as her prick? Another reason to hate this bastard…Wait! This huge guy named Zeke something is talking to the nurse, and even better, Kuster is taking exception, and, even much better, they are squared and Glory, a real fight.

Yes!

That bastard Kuster does have guts but the giant is beating the shit out of him. He's on the floor and Zeke's on top.

A glance around the spectators shows a bunch of mildly excited reptilian stares. Highly trained college graduates are just standing there, no attempt to interfere. Backs are being turned to Kuster's plight. Finally someone says, "Hey Zeke you might hurt your stick hand." And Zeke gets off the evil one and walks out.

Kuster moans a little and bleeds a little then rolls over and staggers up.

"Guess I should have bought him that drink after all."

He looks around for reaction…when he lights on me.

"Huh, Oliver?"

"Buy him a drink, Major? Hell, I thought you were going to buy the farm."

This brings laughter and this brings another brilliant retort.

"What are you doing off the desk?"

"Actually, Major Johnson took me off-something about declining efficiency…sir. Uh, you're bleeding pretty badly, sir."

Slurp.

His nurse tries to wipe his face, but he holds her off. He then mutters something about how he'll talk to Johnson and about how he'll talk to Westerly and about how I'll have no future in the Air Force but that I do have a future on the desk and then he leaves. White male power projection: nothing fired me, nothing got me in more trouble, and nothing made me as uneasy with its tone. The fucking tone was wrong. Yeah…it's a musical problem.

F-4 Night Flight- with all due respect to Richard Bach and Antoine St' Exupery

it's night and the flashing beacons

paint the warriors a macabre red

the whining turns to a muted roar

and a blindless hulk is fed.

MOCK TWO

The only king is the cashiers ring (for Wallace Stevens)

#1

shove the drinks with wooden aplomb

lose that which you can not have

cue up the balls that ivory forgot

jive the juke with drummers salve

2

view crews coming out of the black

bid join the reveries chant

throw knifes into the memorable wall

drink away the warriors cant

CHAPTER 11

Converting Counters for Fun and Survival

In the course of a normal tour, people got their share of scheduled counters and non-counters. The nons being the in country close air support and the Laotian strikes which were mostly at night and often nasty. I called it the Laotian irony, lots of iron but it didn't count for the finish line. The scheduling officer was charged to be fair and get everybody the same rate. In other words everybody that arrived at the same time, departed at approximately the same time. Ah, but in reality there were major differences, because of what aficionados called converting or flipping.

After I decided that the frontseaters were as likely to kill me as the enemy, I had to join this club.

It came about initially as a bomb dump when there was hung ordinance. The idea was to get cleared into PAC One, southern North Vietnam, and try to eject the bomb(s). Then it dawned on some enterprising crew member that it counted as a North ride even if it was only five minutes and five miles over the border. They logged it, the system didn't object and the game was afoot.

And the game had everything a game should have: insider knowledge, danger, creativity, and tangible reward. To convert was to turn a non into a counter. To lessen by one percent the number of times you had to cross the line, literally and figuratively, into the North.

My favorite schemes involved the close air support stuff that was north of Da Nang. It of course involved less time and distance to get from the satisfied customer, the army or marines, to the hallowed ground of PAC One. What I had to find was an agreeable frontseater and he had to be light on the throttle; he had to save fuel. Often times there was ordinance of some kind left, a form or two of destruction not required after we'd blown the shit out of something or other. Say we had bombs and rockets and strafe. The guy on the ground would want a tree line strafed and rocketed, but the bombs wouldn't interest him at all.

"Nope, don't need any bombs today. Too close for those babies. Uh, gotta go now, thanks gunfighter."

The old F-4 milk man is delivering his goods. Yep, the widow Smith wants milk and butter but she doesn't want any cream.

In the south I had even less to do than the north. Mostly because you couldn't see small arms fire trying to hit us. So, I would be recalculating the remaining fuel and the time we had left to get up North and get back home. I could feel the border. It was 50 miles just up the road there. We would be on the deck so there was a sense of unity to the land. We were at crop duster's altitude; belonging to the earth on those close air support rides. Here the north couldn't be seen, only felt. On these rides there wasn't a fucking thing I could do but dream of release by the ground guy and dashing for the count.

"I'm coming baby. I'm coming. Hang on."

"What's that Oliver?"

"Uh, nothing Major. Give me 360 heading and I got the radio."

"Hillsbourgh, this is gunfighter six, over."

"Roger, gunfighter six, go ahead."

"Right, we've got unexpended ordinance. Request clearance to PAC One."

"Roger, gunfighter you've cleared."

Simple as that if you have got the fuel and we do. So we get just above the line and fire or drop whatever and zoom home for the bar. There was no time to find a 'real' target, it was completely fast and meaningless and it fucking counted.

MOCK TWO

The officers club at Da Nang at dawn.

Kromer comes in with a tale of fire and blather.

Seems they got in tight on his bird

Shot out something or other

Non vital, I guess, cause he's still here

Normally you can have country music...

But every thing turns… twists on itself

It's fucking fun to be drunk and safe

listening to American twang in sweat soaked flight suits

we await the next crew to walk in

white salt silhouetting their discarded harnesses

a road map of the sweating terrors

and the strangest kind of award.

CHAPTER 12

Gil's Bloody Short Run

I'm probably going to have to kiss Gil's ass in another life for all the bad-mouthing I've done, but goddammit, Gil, you had some balls, man, you had some. If you were in a singleseater you would have died with some style.

Could have, anyway.

BUT, FUCKER, THERE WAS ANOTHER GUY BEHIND YOU AND HE DESERVED A BETTER GODDAM RIDE OUT OF YOUR ASS THAN HE GOT!!!

The first time I saw Gil Rollie was at a briefing.

It was his first ride in the squadron, and I had drawn him. It's about 40 missions in for me and I'd already seen more than a few types; but here was a new apparition.

Really, he might have been an old ghost dancer. Or a Samurai, like Mushashi but he was...more of a journeyman who's destined to be wiped out early.

He was back at war and he was excited.

I don't think he even wanted to warm up like a good baseball pitcher; he just wanted to come out firing. And how did you tell him much of what he'd been taught, and what he believed, didn't god damn apply?

His unbounded zeal and inexperience followed over his left shoulder like a dangerous giant puppy. A puppy that will probably gobble him up, when it should still be teating.

It was a regular truck hunting mission. Pretty standard ordinance. 500 pound bombs and 20 mm center line Gatling gun.

"Remember that the minimums are 4,500 feet."

I'm trying to get his attention, as I'm saying this, I needed acknowledgement, SOMETHING normal out of this guy.

He's looking off or he's looking right through me.

I continue,

"In the day time, which this is, it's especially important…"

I feel like a fourth grader with a little Johnny, but I can't send him to the principal. Or, he was like the guy who didn't believe in foreplay. I and my wimpy rap bored him. He wanted penetration, he wanted to fuck the North and he didn't care if it was ready for him or not.

All I can do is go into tough assed combat with him and try to save my butt.

We are in the rigging room, putting on our vests when Pete, the other backseater, comes over and starts into our Catch 22 shtick.

"Hey, did Milo sell the chutes yet?"

I answer,

"No, but I've noticed the survival vests look older. You think he's replaced them? Or sold the new ones to the Mig drivers?"

Pete's laughing.

"Let's ask Major Major"

By this time Rollie is looking at us like we're nuts.

"Hey, Captain Rollie."

Pete's putting on his vest, smiling at the guy who will be my latest test in survival.

Rollie's kind of laughing but he doesn't dig it.

The flight.

We get up North okay. The route is called Red and it's quiet, initially. Rollie and I are number Two, following in three mile trail of Lead.

Pete's flying with his regular front guy, a reasonable, survival oriented Major named Harlbot.

Suddenly, the view at 450 knots gets better. Rollie's taken the thing closer to the jungle. I glance at the altimeter. 2,000 feet then 1,500, then 1,000 and…

"What the…"

I stop mid-bitch. The sheer vividness of the scene, the perspective at just above the trees as we screamed along, was mesmerizing.

We went very low in the south all the time, on close air support. But there we had friendliness in some direction if we were hit, if we had to punch out. And there we were working a small piece of turf where the enemy was concentrated, theoretically anyway.

Up here of course everybody hated our guts.

But, it was cool to be that low, after months of staying higher, Rollie's doing his thing and I'm into it and I'm pissed and…

Hey, wait a minute. They can hit us with a rock down here.

Suddenly we blow over a guy on a bicycle. The guy is classic. He looks just like Ho himself. Erect and thin, wispy white beard, he pedals impervious to the savages screaming across the sky above him. You could feel his dignity and his right to be pedaling down a road near his village. It was instant love for me, and I'm straining to get a last look at him when suddenly there are 5 g's on me.

"What's up?" I yell.

It's the first words between us for a long time. Normally, I'm constantly rapping at the frontsters, whether I trust them or not. I want to know what the fuck is up, up there.

"I'm going to get that guy."

Rollie is speaking very calmly, his reptilian brain in complete control.

I'm frantic, in a different way from combat fear. I fear for my pal down there. I got to save him because I know he won't hide. Somehow I know that old man won't get off the road; he would still be there, erect, pedaling, quiet. Somehow I feel like he put me here to see him, to learn.

Maybe if I grab the damn stick and refuse to let go…maybe if I try to use reason…

Wait!

The circuit breakers!!!

I realize I can stop this machine in its killing tracks anytime I want. The little black knobs under the panels in the backseat control every shooting of guns, every dropping of bombs, every firing of rockets. There are about a hundred of them.

Rollie's gotten the beast around, the g's are off and I'm stretched forward trying to find the gun breaker. There!

"You're not going to shoot anyone."

"Why not, Oliver?"

"Because I pulled the fucking gun circuit breaker."

I was calmly talking to him; franticness turned to righteous. I got the fucker and there ain't shit he can do. The insubordination involved will never see its way to the higher ups because Rollie won't say anything. He can't; killing this guy is illegal, at least technically.

How could this be, anyway? How the hell could two highly trained young American males be trolling for targets in a strange land in a brilliant machine made dirty by its camouflage. And how the hell could one of them want to kill an old bicycle rider and the other one feel tenderness for him? And how the hell could this act of mercy by one of these white males be anything compared to the destruction in which he has already participated?

I didn't know then and I don't know now, but God, it matters. It did and it does. I've fantasized about that guy since, dreamed about meeting him, walking with him in his fields. He would be the wisdom of the ancient culture we were ravaging. Smoking a pipe, he would signal me to his hut.

His eyes.

I can't see his eyes. But his eyes do the talking.

"What right did you have to even be in the place to prevent my slaughter?"

"None. But I did have the power and I used it."

"Maybe I was suffering and wanted to be killed."

"Nobody wants to be machine-gunned on a road."

He smiles and I smile at him and bow, as he gently waves me away.

But, now suddenly Rollie drops all pretense of balance.

Lower and lower we get, until we're scraping the trees. Rollie's raging against my recalcitrance, my doubt.

He's trying to scare me to death.

I figure it's over. We're too close, too low. I'm looking up at huts built on slight rises. There's a bomb crater, brown water with small choppy waves. There's a village with a woman and child looking at us, there's someone aiming a rifle way in front of the beast.

The little irony is I should have died after saving someone; the big irony is we will be saved by being hit. It felt like three taps, bumps that moved us sideways. Yes, the 40 thousand pound monster can be shaken; can be slid across the sky by small hostile bits of lead.

This seemed to also snap Rollie out of it, like a Zen bullet smacking the student.

"What was that?" he asks.

"That was a love tap; you've really made some friends today. I think we got hit"

Warning lights are coming on, utility hydraulics, electrical… The red pieces of glowing plastic seemed to be more meaningful to Gil than all that preceded it, for we started up. And I mean up. All fighter pilots look for altitude, there's safety in air underneath you, however temporary it may be.

The wounds, however severe, didn't keep us from climbing. Especially after Rollie blows off all ordinances.

"Let's head south, Captain. And call Lead."

As I say these words, it dawns on me that we just might make this after all. Whatever damage had occurred, the thing is responding and it's the usual fifteen minutes home. I'm never happy in the North but I'm literally squirming in the seat, so energized to still be alive with this maniac.

Lead confirmed some damage on the fuselage.

"You've got a couple of holes. Not very big. How's the flying?"

"It's handling fine."

Rollie's using the "everything's cool, especially me," voice.

"Utility hydraulics light is on."

Lead tells us to expect to blow down the landing gear, and that we have no brakes, no nose wheel steering, and limited rudder.

Thanks a lot Lead, but I'd already read that shit in the emergency book. I can read real fast when my ass depends on it.

When we get near Da Nang, the usual emergency is declared.

Emergency landings in peacetime were a big deal, fire trucks with flashing lights, ambulances, Jeeps, even the Tower would be excited.

Here it was standard procedure, almost. It was impossible to see much difference with the level of activity at Da Nang, for at that moment it was the most crowded airstrip in the world, late '67.

Still, the subgods were damaged and the dubious deities wanted to come home NOW!

The problem with our chariot was twofold. One was diminished lateral control. Without complete rudder control, the ability to keep it rolling straight down the runway becomes problematic. Nose wheel steering is also handy, at times. Normally used for taxi, it can be employed in extreme drifts. And there's the matter of stopping without brakes. If Rollie could keep it on the concrete long enough, we would hit the barrier at the other end, twelve thousand feet down.

But the same gimmick that almost killed me and the Hopple, the cable system, can now be used to help save me and this idiot.

Rollie drops the hook and lands just before the cable.

Presto.

The wounded one does the famous carrier quirk lurch, then stops.

And it's over. When I pop the canopy, even the drenched, steaming Da Nang air felt like liquid velvet.

As I climb down over the wing, a couple of rescue guys are smiling. A sort of "welcome home, gee you guys are great" kind of thing. Their normalcy is touching and I crack them up.

"Gee, how nice of you guys to come to our little get together, especially on such short notice and everything."

One guys grins back.

"No problem, Lieutenant. And you sure picked a nice spot."

"Yeah we were really lucky to get this space. You normally have to reserve halfway down the right runway far in advance."

"Looks like someone don't like you, sir."

One of the guys is gesturing towards the holes.

"Can you blame them?"

As I say this, Rollie finally climbs out of the frontseat.

I walk over to him. He has a supercilious little grin, as if a little joke had just been played.

"You're a dead man, Rollie. I don't know when but you're meat. I'll never get in one of these things with you again. Period. And it makes me sick that someone else has to ride with you."

Specter like, he looks at me. Over his shoulder I can see the hydraulic fluid dripping on the runway, forming a blood red pool.

CHAPTER 13

Bond and the Boys

Each Squadron is divided into three flights. This means very little except as a chain of command deal.

If there is a problem, it requires the proper shuffle through one's flight commander. So I go to see a cat named Major Bond, a husky pipe smoker who gives off an enlightened wrestler vibe.

"What's the problem, Oliver?"

"Well, the main problem is I'm in the backseat. But the more specific immediate deal is this guy Rollie."

"You guys got tapped yesterday, huh?"

"Yeah. I'm not sure if it was bullets or some kid throwing rocks."

Bond's eyebrow goes up behind the smoke.

"Listen, Maj, the way he flew today there's no way he clocks a hundred. Hell, to be a little macabre, I'd bet he doesn't make twenty."

Bond leans back, thinking.

"So what do you want to do?"

"It's what I don't want to do. I don't want to fly with him… ever again"

"You realize this could be reflected on your OER"

"Does that mean if I kept flying with him, you would send a good OER in the pine box with my body. My Mother could frame it over the mantel. On second thought, there wouldn't be a body would there? We seem to have a shortage of bodies. Plenty of death, but no bodies."

"That's enough. Lieutenant. You won't have to fly with him again."

Walking out of there, I almost felt like the stinking tour was over. So I go straight to the bar. That was the ticket.

In a long afternoon and evening of drinking the word spread.

Montague and Kromer and Moffitt and Waters and more, all the cool backseaters wanted to hear what I had done.

"It's fucking unprecedented."

Kromer is throwing his ranger knife into the wall and grinning. He's got 80 missions North and has seen even more crap than the rest of us.

I make a speech,

"Hereafter I shall be called comrade Oliver, your cell leader. If the fellow travelers in the frontseat of the peoples' airplane don't obey the honorable directives of the commissars, we want to hear about it. So, any time a new guy arrives to risk our asses with his own, a 'people of the backseat' panel will be convened. Here we will discuss the merits and shortcomings of the new aircraft commander."

"And what the hell will you accomplish?"

It's one of the southern idiots, of course. Some clown named Hatfield, who has all the earmarks of the half-bright R.O.T.C. dink, has wandered over.

"How about INCREASED SURVIAL RATES, Hatfield?"

"You know Oliver, Ah can't believe you graduated from the Air Force Academy. Ah really can't."

I had another drink of gin. Just like Camus, I sought its compassion giving power. This was too important to just tweak the redneck.

"Listen, Hatfield, there's something else you can't believe if you want to get back to the land of Lyndon. You can't believe all these ace's will bring you home, 'cause some of them will airmail your ass to hell."

"Ah will fly with who they tell me to."

"Hey, Hatfield you ended a sentence with a preposition, which is better than ending your life with a bad proposition."

And with that Hatfield storms out. And with that a queasy feeling comes over me.

Damn it, Hatfield.

You got a weird dark aura around you. I want you to make it, I want you to go home and vote Republican and have little Hatfields and run your wife's daddy's business, or fly airlines…

I don't want you to get blown up because of some other fucker's fantasy.

CHAPTER 14

Kromer Delivers a Eulogy

Two weeks after Rollie and I got hit, Kromer was Number One on a night mission in PAC One, north of Dong Hoi.

"The weather sucked," said Kromer. "We should have canceled. But we went to take a look, anyway. Fuck, man, it was storming on the coast. Lightning and gusty winds. It was funny though, because the ceiling was…about 3,000… 3,500 feet, pretty high. It was the beach that defined the real mean area. The Major asked me what I thought and I said screw it, but he said let's take a closer look, maybe we can punch through. We couldn't. It started getting lower and meaner. Rollie and Hatfield were in trail. When we pulled off and before we could call him, Rollie comes up on the radio, says he sees an opening and he's going to try to get under.

"I thought it was fucked…Get under for what?"

"We turned back south; I was looking out the right rear when I saw a flash that couldn't have been lightning. It was a different color. Not white: it was red and yellow."

Kromer looks up from his drink, glances at my eyes, and shakes his head.

"It was as senseless a loss as I can remember. Talk about sound and fury."

"Who was in the backseat?"

I ask.

"Hatfield."

"Fuck."

Kromer had gone to some literary school back east. We used to exchange books for those occasional nights when we weren't drinking.

He lifts the mug that he always drank from.

"Here's to the ones that won't see home. And here's to the ones who die all alone. And here's to pilots who can actually fly. And here's to the ones that help you die. Here's to the fruits of rotten hegemony. And here's to my girlfriend's lovely alimony."

I laughed and asked who she was.

"She's a beauty who married for money the first time and now she wants the fighter pilot stick."

"I guess you have to be a real knife thrower to get a woman like that, huh?"

"Well you can't be a wiseass, edgy, survival driven weirdo, one who isn't near respectful enough of his military superiors."

"I didn't know you saw me so clearly. Did you hear anything after the fireball?"

"Nothing, except the Major bitching about Rollie going that way. I hope Hatfield was...fuck. You knew it; you knew Rollie was a maniac. Listen. I'm almost done but you can try to stop some of this stuff.

"Count on it."

In the two weeks between my encounter with Rollie and his demise, there had been no new frontseaters but several were due in. And since it was no secret what I had predicted, a strange power came to me.

Suddenly, I was akin to a shaman foreteller.

CHAPTER 15

Save Your Ass Club

"Everybody has their own criteria in this insanity, but if the new guy flies in any way that is officially unauthorized, you don't have to go with his ass."

There are a couple of incredulous looks at this sedition, but most of the people around the table are very seriously listening to Joe Moffitt, who has taken to this concept with fervor.

"You know that Oliver refused Rollie's ride and you know what happened. There's one little problem with a guy doing that unless we stick together. SOME OTHER FUCKER HAS TO GO!!"

I know now that this act of defiance was part of the tremor rolling through the culture. At the time, all I knew was some other guys were supporting my move, and I did not feel so alone.

Harley Harrison walks in, sees us and comes over shaking his head.

"Just took my second ride with Johannsen. Today we went south on a close air. We were supposed to lay down napalm on a ridgeline. The army was trying to take the fucking thing, I guess. Uh…gotta get a drink."

As he orders, Moffitt says,

"Shit, close air. What could he have done that…?"

"It's what he didn't do. He didn't listen."

Hacket is sliding back to the table and talking while glancing over his shoulder to see if any fronties are looking.

"I've been on 60 rides, he's been on zip. The first pass he fucks up the switches, after I called them off like a good soldier. The second pass he gets the cans off and misses way long because he was too damn fast. I told him that fast was usually better than slow but it's nice to hit the target instead of friendlies. He tells me to knock it off, Lieutenant. He's in charge. Then Col. Parness, in the other plane…he finally gets some on the enemy."

Harrison looks off at the jukebox. Nobody says a word. Testifying was taken seriously. When a guy let go, it was understood that you let him finish. Our nervous systems were at stake, though we probably didn't think of it in those terms.

Harley slams his beer can on the table.

"Fuck, I hate napalm."

I love him for saying it.

Our wing had to carry that shit a lot in the south.

Napalm was made out of aluminum beer cans, stuffed with explosive gel; they are cigar shaped, slimy products of human ingenuity. They didn't curve parabolically, like a nice bomb. No, they tumbled, rolled - all axis incoherent - to a self-pyre. Glinting in the sun then losing the light then glinting again, they strike earth and ignite.

Sucking air selfishly they kill themselves and everything in their swath. It was no mistake that the monks chose fire to try to tell us. We chose fire as an answer. Although come to think of it, what good are monks, anyway? They ain't got no money.

Harley continues,

"Now today me and Johanssen go north, trying to stop the evil ones from coming south and leaving their empty ammo cans on pristine, free beaches. I go through the usual jive. 45 will keep you alive. Does he listen? Hell no. Indeed he's all over the place on one run. He can't get the pipper on the target, so he presses to three thousand before he pulls. And of course he's long."

When dive-bombing it was crucial to drop at the altitude prescribed or the big bang goes awry.

"What are you going to do with this guy, Harley?"

Harley did the Roman thing thumbs down. And the rebellion gathered itself. One by one the thumbs went down.

Insubordination is a rare thing in any officer corps. We were walking a fine line, a couple of the fronties looked at us over their drinks. Like any ruling class they can sense the peons plotting. This insurrection has a nice caveat, though. If the front can hack it talent wise and will listen to the back, especially the more experienced backseaters, there's no problem. At least on that plane of existence there was no problem…

It was for many of us a sort of early new-age lesson in sexual politics. We were two pilots, just like a marriage is two lovers. There must be some sense of equality or it's just a typical bullshit hierarchy. All we fledgling Save Your Ass Club members were doing was preparing for divorce. Some of my highfalutin' friends have always wondered why I love sports. Of course the short answer is that to a usually large degree the best rise to the top. An extreme meritocracy is major league baseball. All we were trying to do here was have a chance. It was kind of like spring training. We ain't taking every clown they throw at us, they have to be coachable, and they have to co-operate or get lost.

They could still fly some minor league thing-just not the beast and just not with the Save Your Ass Club.

The idea flew. We moved Johannsen, or the commander did when no one in our group would go up with him. Kicked his ass upstairs to Saigon. Bye. No regrets. It probably, no, almost undoubtedly, saved his ass and one of us.

Mechanics

the beast tenders usually got it right

for without their succor the fight would stop

they fed her, bathed her, and loaded her

they hailed the riders and wondered what it was like

and the riders went out in small cabals

not the large conspiracies of euro drops

and one beast tender dared to speak to me his burning desire

to ride the ride

and I wanted to tear off my battle gear

and place it gently on him

and kiss his helmeted head

On a friend getting hit over A Shau Valley, punching out and calling in a strike on his own head

#1

BOMB me BOMB me

the radio throbbed.

its better to vaporize

than suffer a thousand knives

#2

I can not drop

said the cop up top

for this i can not abide

killing my own pleading side

#3

wait! you fucker I screamed

my pain will fuse glass hatred for you

who couldn't kill my love

you let him suffer so you wouldn't have to.

CHAPTER 16

Everyone's a Backseater

Kromer's drunk, I'm drunk but it's in that era when everything is crystalline, obvious, and brilliant.

"One way or another everyone's a backseater," Kromer slurs. "Someone else is always in control whether you are a wife, employee, kid, even the freakin' president, because if nothing else the frontseater in everybody's life is death or fate. Both can crash our asses at anytime. So, when we are in the goddamn plane we are triple cursed. Control at one level is the frontseater, who has very little control himself, then there are the gunners who can be, with a little bad luck, in charge, then there is our own terror.

It's a multiple layer of crap, disguised by the technical brilliance of the machine, and our denial of some or most of what I just said."

CHAPTER 17

The Broken Lance

It started when Baggins and I were in Formosa, flying a bird to a repair base. The first thing to do upon return was always to ask if anyone had gone down.

Someone had.

It had been a night mission. Lead was hosed by a 37-millimeter stream in Laos. Two said it looked like a flaming candle subscribing an arc across the black. They also agreed, the guys in Two, that nobody could have made it out. It happened too fast and the flames were engulfing.

The backseater in Lead was a classmate, Lance Sijan. He was a big football kind of guy whom I hadn't known well at school, but he had an unusual artistic ability. He was a brilliant wood sculptor; one or two of his works are still at the Academy, I hear. I hear they named a building after him. I'll thank them for you, Lance.

Thanks.

I was scheduled on a morning mission approximately 30 hours after the crash. This mission happened to be going near the crash scene. As soon as I read the mission statement I had this haunting feeling, it was palpable, and I couldn't get rid of it.

Lance had made it out.

A guy named Lee was the other backseater on Lance's mission. At least he was a drinker and I could find him easily. Bar stool to bar stool, he's looking like I'm full of it.

It's late the night before my next mission and I'm drunk but the feeling is strong as ever.

"But how the fuck do you know nobody made it?" I demand.

Lee shakes his head.

"Nobody could have made it, man. It was a freaking fireball."

"Yeah, but your description of a curving flight path…"

Lee just shook his head.

"We stayed as long as we could, until bingo. There were no beepers. They bought it, Oliver. Sorry."

He paused.

"It was really hot. I mean there were a lot of 37s and it was closer than it should have been. A couple of 57s too and Joe, my frontseater was a little spooked and so was I. With what I hear about the Pathet Lao, it's the worst place in the whole damn theater."

Theater? You call this a theater; I call it a fucking cauldron.

Lee's all right but I'm hoping he's all wrong.

Next morning, through my hangover, I shake hands with a frontseater who was a decent guy named Carlson.

"Uh, look, major, that bird that went down the night before last, we're going near the spot today. I would like to divert a little and go right over it."

"How do you know where it is?"

"Two got the inertial nav coordinates before leaving. I'll put them in and if the fucker's working right we should be close."

"Okay, Oliver, it can't hurt."

Hurt? Hurt's the name of this whole game, pal.

But there's something. It's funny, but I did not want my intuition working during the war. It's too close to other brain forms, not conscience exactly, something else that I don't want to confront. Not now, not in the war. Later maybe.

It's real, this feeling about Lance; and I must shake it and this ride will do it.

After takeoff, we spread way wide of Lead, probably six or seven miles on his right.

Steaming at about 5,000 feet, heading northwest towards Laos, Lead went in and out of sight, playing with the clouds.

Laos has mountains with formations called Karst, apparently caused by limestone erosion. It was the nastiest looking stuff I'd ever seen and the inertial nav leads us right towards it.

"Turn five degrees right, we're coming up on the spot."

Carlson turns, I look off the left at the looming mountains, and look back at the inertial just as it hits the zero point and Lance comes up on his radio!

"This is Omaha Two. Do you read?"

A surge of electricity sweeps through me. Perhaps never in the whole damn dance of life have I felt like that, but the thrill was accompanied by an anxiety and the profound sense that I was limited in my ability to further influence events.

Combat is like that; you are powerful and constrained at the same time.

"It's Lance. It's Sijan. He's down there." I'm yelling.

It's spooky to hear someone you know on a little radio way below, someone who was just like you a day and a half ago, young and powerful and fast.

Then to be jolted by hostile steel and see flames all around and reach between your legs and pull a little handle and float in a black jungle sky hearing the plane's howl and hearing guns croaking their desire for your wingman who's circling helplessly above.

Then you smash into trees, or rocks, or karst, or stream or whatever breaks your leg and sends the impulse to scream onto your brain.

You can hear your heartbeat. You can hear your breathing. You can hear your fear. Then you hear your wingman depart and the natural sounds of the jungle reclaim the night. And you're left in pain and fear.

Carlson cranks a sharp turn and below we look at what became, in the next two days, the site of the biggest rescue effort in the history of the war…

Sijan has a broken leg and he'd already been down for a night and a day and another night. Alone…hiding from hunters. Moving in pain, moving by crawling probably. Waiting for help, waiting for flights, and they didn't come the first day, not fucking close enough. The second night he's hiding, sweating, and in serious pain. The morning finally arrives and he hears jets coming closer, then right over him, and he's got a chance.

Later after the freaking war I started to read a book about this thing and the author says it was a flight from Thailand that first picked up Lance's radio call. Not true pal. It was us. Not that I give a shit for any credit, but it was his own wing that tried to save him. So fuck you for getting it wrong.

We tried, Lance.

We circled until the first rescue chopper with A-1 support appeared.

The A-1 was a huge single engine prop refugee from WWII that was distinguished by its ability to fly for many hours and carry enormous quantities of weapons.

This one, however, had little time to show off its capabilities for it was shot down almost immediately.

The rescue chopper picked up the A-1 pilot and departed.

Another time Lance hears possible salvation slowly fade.

We were relieved soon after that by the PAC 6 Thailand flights before another rescue effort was mounted.

The effort went all day and into the night before Lance was captured by the Pathet Lao.

Hundreds of sorties were flown to no avail trying to pick him up.

Sometimes they got close but always the ground fire became overwhelming and the choppers had to withdraw.

Back at Da Nang, a few days later a stewardess friend of Lance walks into his squadron's flight shack looking for him.

The silence that followed spoke to centuries of the ultimate uselessness of language in the face of needless, young loss.

MOCK TWO

On vacationing with a Chinese lady of the night in the middle of war

Taipei got the best hookers, he said

let us phantom over and relax

i wondered if such a thing was possible

to go from remote killing to remote fucking

in a flash of afterburner time

to replace the black movie

with a blue movie

to awaken with a silken youngster

nineteen i think she was

who perplexed over my nonperformance

suffered with me

til i sent her home stuffed with dollars

and lay alone

and wondered who died while i was away

CHAPTER 18

The Day the Chief Went Down

I'm honored.

I hear Faust is giving me a ride with Socks. Gee, it's great. Maybe I'll put on a clean flight suit. It's obvious he's a jerk but there's a curiosity about any real, famous old timer. He flew in Korea and did get some Migs and he certainly has the bluster. Hey, if a guy can back it up, it's cool. Someone asked Gerry Mulligan, the great white saxophone player, about race and jazz. He said something like if a cat can blow he can blow whether he's black, white, or green.

In this dance there's little correlation between external ego and talent. A dude can be a raving asshole and really incapable of bending the beast at the edge. Or he can be quiet and unassuming and kick ass at six g's. Or he can be a washed up old ham fist. Never know.

It was a day flight to Laos, and a seemingly standard ride with a FAC on the Ho Chi Minh trail. When we get there I'm thinking the gunners may have been on lunch break. We didn't see them shooting, and the FAC was trying to be funny.

"Hey gunfighter. Welcome to my office complex. If you look at the clearing just west of you, you'll see a pock marked reddish area with a stream flowing through it. I would like you to clean up my park. There's been some illegal parking going on. They're not paying rent and I want them evicted."

"Roger, we got it."

Socks has a bored quality in his voice.

I can dig boredom; but on an airplane doing combat in freakin' Laos? This strikes me as Samurai shit that has gone too far.

Socks tells Two to go in 30 seconds after us and we roll over from about ten thousand. It's then that I realize this guy is not using a 45-degree dive or anything short of straight down. And I mean fucking straight down, which feels bizarre and is conducive to hitting absolute nothing. Which is what he hits, on top of which he's rough as hell and snatches about seven g's on my ass.

When I recover my ability to see, I glance down to note the bombs way long in the rough.

Bad drive, Colonel. That's a penalty stroke, except you can't tee up another one today-no more balls.

The FAC comes on, a little ennui in his voice.

"Well, maybe they'll pay up. I'm sure they heard those babies hit somewhere."

FAC's were often kind of wiseasses. They were alone and maybe a little batty, flying around slowly, looking for something to kill. But not directly, no, not direct killing, but by voice and command. The whole damn war had floating birds of prey, praying for targets, praying for time, praying for luck.

It's at this point that the radio starts screaming.

"Gunfighter One is down. Gunfighter One is down..."

"Oh my god," says Socks. "The chief's been hit. The chief is down."

Apparently Wing Commander O'Sullivan was also flying and had trouble. Socks is really shook. The plane is moving all over the place, and we were heading for Da Nang fast.

The lowly FAC was forgotten as well as his factitious target. Socks hardly thanked the man for the game.

Hell, man, the Chief was down. Of course the irony is that a pilot had to first rise in his exploding seat before he falls. Up like a rocket ship that fails orbit, then floating over monolithic color, green or blue, jungle or ocean.

Two calls and asks us what's happening.

All Socks says is he has to get to base. We still have rockets, but apparently Socks thinks he can do something more important than the fucking mission because he blows it off.

"The Chief's down."

Yeah, I gather that, Socks. What about the backseater? You think he might be down too? Huh? Do you give a shit? I can't stand this jerk. He keeps mumbling and I got my hand an inch from the stick in case this clown passes out from anxiety.

I say, "Yes, sir, this is really bad. We just have to get safely back to Da Nang and find out what's happening." The subtext of my rap was: let's not try to kill ourselves by mourning before this thing is on the ground, the drag chute billowing its gladness behind my butt.

"The Chief's down."

Jesus.

Finally, Two shows up on the right wing. I look wistfully over, and wave at them. Then I do the old rotating hand with my index finger pointing at my helmet.

Skip, the backseater, gives me the stroking one index finger with the other. It was naughty boy stuff. We're real clever on these missions.

It's possible to follow the rescue on the radio, sort of, because part of the dialogue is on guard channel. This is a channel that the radios are tuned to, in addition to our own discreet frequency. Sometimes guard channel is like listening to a soap opera.

But then the rescue goes to a different frequency and it's just Socks and me.

"Where were they flying today, colonel?"

"What. Oh, he went to PAC One. Uh, don't bother me. I've got to think this through."

Okay dipshit. I figure you're thinking the "what if the command is mine" scenario. That would be cool. Replacing a pepped up egomaniac with a completely incompetent one might be interesting. Maybe you'll give a seminar on dive-bombing, followed by some Korean reminiscences. Then we can all jump to attention when you leave, renewed and full of fervor for the fight.

It's funny how that never happened. No speeches. No visits by the brass in my whole tour. It was a class thing me thinks. No need to slum with the common soldiers. I mean the generals had to run around having meetings, talking about useless targets we didn't hit, having long lunches, schmoozing junketing congressmen, shit like that. It was foretelling, like much else in the war, of the new America. Gone were the Omars and Pattons, replaced with the Mandarin overlords. Pretty boy idiots like Westy were cosmetic generals.

The new Air Force Chief of Staff had never been in command of a wing of any kind in his whole slippery career. He had been a staff weenie the entire boogie; his career dance was away from the messy details and risks of actual fliers. The new America demanded a different currency, if not green blessings then facial ones. New levels of superficiality were emerging between the bombs.

The landing goes without incident though I remain vigilant. Socks quits talking. Maybe the eulogy is being written.

As we taxi in, Socks starts in on the Chief again.

"He's down…"

He's taxiing fast for the stalls when he suddenly stops and wheels the Phantom right at a disgorging airliner.

What?

"Look at that stew." Socks waxes. "Look at her man…would I like to get her ass in the sack. See what you can do for me, will you Lieutenant?"

I put my mask back on, slide my visor down and hunker lower, eager not to be seen. In fact the only thing I'm eager to do is get straight to the bar. This is worse than being shot at.

The stew solves my problem by turning her back on us and going into the airliner. Apparently she's not impressed with an idling, steaming jet fighter; noxious fumes roiling out of its butt, and a bobbing, panting helmet leering from its frontseat.

Socks wheels the machine and taxis it into its spot, sheathed by walls of steel and sand bags. There is a wing toady waiting for old number Two and they dash off, in anxious intercourse. I take my time getting out, pissed that this thing didn't count except for the story; I already got plenty of bar currency raps. I… want… counters. Counters. Counters make me feel a little better…well, no not better exactly but stronger and less fragile and a bit more scared and a little hopeful.

Sort of.

The squadron room has the business as usual feel; so I have to ask someone about the mighty leader and his backseater.

"They picked them up from the water and they both survived. The colonel was hurt."

"That's it?"

I want some more details but the bird was from a different squadron and nobody knows anything else.

About this time a dreaded thing happens. Some clown backseater named Holoperick comes up.

"Oliver, you haven't been writing any medal missions. There's plenty of work, describing stuff that has happened. It will help your OER if you show some initiative and get on the old typewriter, you know. Major Clark told me the other day that it was difficult to distinguish backseaters unless we show some individual…"

I hold up my hand to silence this patter. It's a big thing, embellishing war stories to get guys more decorations. Sometimes it looks like an old newspaper office, typewriters clattering away with that strange mixture of truth and fiction so apropos to the American dream.

"Stop right there, Lieutenant. You don't know this but I am doing serious research every day - in addition to my important backseat duties, of course. Those are paramount to the winning effort we are all engaged in. But I'm also doing a careful analysis of the other participants who show themselves in this fascinating nexus of American effort. And in fact I'm headed for that underrated forum of discussion: the bar. Later."

As I walk in, Kromer is standing in a circle of guys, laughing his ass off.

"What's up?"

He points at the centerpiece of the action. The backseater Ted Guaranik is standing in a dripping-wet flightsuit and appears to be the lucky one who down went with the chief.

"This guy's a riot. Here's the story. Apparently O'Sullivan told everybody including the mechanics that he was going to get that pesky quad 50 shooter at Dong Hoi. You know that fucker has hit three planes but nobody went down yet. So he was damn tired of getting his boys shot up and it was time to settle that fuckers hash. He boldly took himself up there to finish 'that little dink' once and for all."

It should be noted again that to hunt guns for their own sake was officially frowned upon. Certainly unofficially by the Save Your Ass Club and myself. It was self-defeating as their job, the gunners, was to kick our ass or scare us into bad bombing, get us to go after them instead of a 'useful' target. But the old Colonel decided to go outside that logic. It was almost a noblesse oblige kind of thing,

"I'm king and shall slay the dragon that you commoners aren't allowed to touch."

And as is often the case, the royalty is full of shit colored hubris. The gunner brought number one and his reluctant sidekick to their mach two blues.

"Guaranik says they got hit at about 3,000 feet right after pickle, in a turn towards the water."

I say, "At least O'Sullivan had that figured out. Turning to the sea. All F-4s are happier dying in the sea. After all they were born of the navy. And their riders are happier not having to run through the jungle and scuff up their feet."

"Imagine if that fucker with the quads could see the bombs falling towards him as he shot the shit out of the attacker. Cool."

Kromer got the gleam in his eye.

I suddenly have this love for that NVA cat up there. Hell, he's only seventy or eighty miles from here. It's about as far as Philly is from New York. We could get in a Jeep and drive up to salute him, get drunk with him, and try to sign him to a baseball contract. Anyone that could hit a streaking hostile fighter might kick shit out of a mere baseball.

"I hope they didn't get the quad man. I've got plans for him."

"This gets Kromer laughing and one of the fronts from Guaranik's squadron turns from the throng and says,

"What plans are those, Lieutenant?"

"Well, I'd like to get that evil fucker myself, Major."

"I've heard of you, Oliver. You're lucky I'm not your superior. I don't like your attitude."

"Well, better a bad attitude than a bad altitude…sir."

Now Kromer is really rocking and the missionary leaves the savages to their attempts in forming a new tribe. Somehow we knew we needed a ceremony. Somehow we knew we weren't going to get it.

The colonel went around the base with a huge brace on his neck for several weeks, unwilling to relinquish command. Finally, the great powers called him home.

"Yes, losing him is like losing hydraulic fluid. There's a little less rudder around here."

Thus Kromer had the final word.

As always.

To the Mig 15

your first dance was Korea

where the Northern kids who rode you

didn't know they were conning

white trails off your gorgeous tail

beckoning the older gangs of american killers

exactly where to put their white hot shots

CHAPTER 19

Rocket and the Monk

Rocket and the Monk were feeling good with a capital damn G.

Rocket is standing at the bar, which was where he has insisted they bring him upon delivery by rescue chopper. It was a very short ride.

He's one of my favorites. A little blond guy with a strange macabre sense of the dance he found himself in.

"There wasn't much stirring in Laos and the FAC was low on fuel."

Rocket's testifying.

"We dove down on some dusty road and unloaded all the bombs on a pass each. Some light 37 mills that weren't even close. Said goodbye and head home. I tell the Monk he must be living right; maybe those drunken benedictions he's always giving me at three in the morning are working."

I say, "Well, somebody has to be the spiritual leader of the drunks."

Rocket laughs and says,

"There's more than one head priest drinker around here. Anyway we get back here and there's a north wind so it's the southern approach over the river. We were in standard three mile trail of Lead and starting on the descent, gear down, when it felt like somebody was beating on the side of the fuselage with a hammer, wham, wham…and all hell breaks loose. I was looking at the hole in the canopy and thinking the fresh air feels strange, never felt fresh air on a ride before when Monk yells 'Get out! Get out!' and I grabbed the top handle and prayed the plane wasn't too low and pulled hard. The damn seat got me out. Next thing I remember is looking down at the freaking river to my right and the base to my left. I was pissed off. Fuck it if you ain't safe on final for Christ sakes."

Now the Monk walks over, even muddier, and puts his arm around Rocket and takes over the dialogue.

"When my chute opened it felt like I was 50 feet off the ground. Then the bird hit and it was like the world's most expensive flare going off. Then I could see I actually had a few hundred feet, and I looked over my shoulder and saw Rocket. He was close and I looked back towards the base and saw the tower lights flashing, then I looked back for Rocket when I hit…Hard. I got up and started to yell at him when all hell broke loose, from heavy small arms fire. They were on the south side of the river; we were on the north. It wasn't enough to get the plane; they wanted both of us as a kind of trifecta. Then it gets quiet and I started to climb up when Audie Murphy here fires off his pistol at them. Jesus, they opened up on our asses… What the hell was your idea, pal?"

Rocket speaks, "I'll tell you what I was doing. I was exchanging fire with the enemy while you had your face in the mud."

"Then why did you go running past me towards the base after they lit up the sky the second time?"

"Well," Rocket gets a little grin on. "I had done enough exchanging for one night."

The Rocket was a kindred spirit and I respected his man the Monk.

It was sweet to see them bantering. It was sweet to see them, period. One of those moments of shared joy when somebody you respect and love makes it back from riding the iron chair, when there's a save, when someone has to leave the beast in mid-flight and is dragged, pulled or roped back, wet and glowing with post-ejection bliss...

Then you sensed the grace that some had and no one had...

CHAPTER 20

Rocket Attack

ROCKET ATTACK!!!

Man, they were at it again. It seemed like it was usually about 4 am, the hour of the wolf; the hour when more men die of heart attacks than any other. What better time to try to kill the pilots in their repose, or at least scare the hell out of them?

When they started to blow, I would crawl down the hall to Jerry Cliff's room. A huge guy for a fighter pilot, he had been an all American fullback from one of the football factories in the south. It became a tradition, he and I drinking during rocket attacks. He'd be on the floor with a bottle of Johnny Walker and two glasses.

"Can you imagine those little bitty guys slowly, slowly sneaking those things through the security of this wonderful establishment? Setting them up, God knows how, to hit this hallowed hall."

Jerry would be smiling.

I would pick it up.

"Yeah, Jerry, Something like maybe the Alabama boys would have done to your football dorm if they'd had the ordinance."

Jerry and I were drinking bar buddies, unusual for the fact that he was a frontseater. I had flown with him and thought he was competent.

Once, he and I had been drinking all night when another pilot came in at daybreak and looked at us like we were insane. Seems we had been scheduled for a dawn test pilot ride. We were both stinking drunk. We staggered to a quick breakfast and headed for the plane. The thing seemed beautiful through my crystalline vision. It looked like fun. Jerry was whistling the Georgia Tech fight song. We were okay until the end of the runway when Jerry pulled off his mask, leaned over the side of the cockpit and barfed down the side of the fuselage.

"Gee, Jerry I'm glad you didn't do that on takeoff roll."

He was quiet for a minute and he said,

"What the hell are we doing over here anyway?"

A question being asked by millions, being summed up by my half sick pal.

Merriment had turned to morosement.

Now, as the rockets threatened, we always listened to the Seekers, a music group whose big hit went like, "close the door, light the light, I'll be home tonight."

He had the speakers blowing their stuff through the whole damn building.

"Far away from the hustle and bustle and bright city lights…"

Jerry drank and began slipping into a rap about his wife. Actually the subject really was his infidelities.

"Ah love her Ron. Ah love her a lot. We go stepping a lot. Dancing, man. Drinking. Fine dining.'

"That sounds cool, Jerry."

"She loves me and it doesn't matter."

"What doesn't matter?"

"The other girls. Ah, screw around. But it don't mean nothing, it don't."

I could never bring myself to ask if she knew. Here was a guy who had fulfilled not one but two of the great American male fantasies, on the verge of breaking down. He was a sweet cat who cared enough to be in pain.

Hope you're still stepping with your lady somewhere, Jerry. Hope you've forgiven yourself, for indiscretions big and small.

CHAPTER 21

Kelley Mahoney

I walked into the bar, and there's Kelly Mahoney.

Shit.

The guy was my squadron officer in charge at the blue zoo. That's a commissioned officer that had a squadron of cadets to look after and I for one needed a lot of attention.

I'm at 75 missions north and feeling melancholy and nervous and I really liked Kelly. I'm hoping he's just visiting from headquarters or something. He was the guy who shepherded me through school. He told me later, there was one bad boy he tried to keep in school from every class and I was it for '65. He was loyal, he had Irish soul, and dammit he was an actual old time fighter jock before his AFA assignment.

I had that feeling again. That feeling of pre-dread like the future can be emotionally implied. My psychic abilities were increasing. I was being pushed forward by the whole fucking thing as a way to see, to portend. It was weird and strange and kind of grey. Dammit, I didn't fucking like Kelly's chances.

He was old, 40 or so, and I didn't want him here. I wanted him safe.

He was like my uncle, really. He cared about me. He liked the rascals like me because he was an old Irish warrior soul. Very loving.

"How's it going, Oliver?"

"Uh, it's pretty tough, Colonel."

He smiled back at me, brave and lonely and excited.

Soon after, one night at Da Nang, Kelly asked me about the time when I was almost thrown out of school, an episode he, ironically, admired.

Bob Dylan was coming to Denver on his first tour west of the Mississippi in 1964.

I was an admirer of his muse, an unpopular stance in an institution that loved Ayn Rand.

Anyway, I had no privileges coming, and was unauthorized to leave school on that fateful Saturday night.

As usual I had committed academic sub-performance.

I decided to skip out and take my chances, even though this was a big no-no at school. My buddy Gus Johnson got us a ride to Denver but we had no ride home. We figured we'd hitchhike and take our chances.

The concert was at the University of Denver.

It was amazing. Dylan had that young genius aura oozing out from every Levi-covered pore.

We made it back to a southbound on ramp, when a classmate from school fortuitously stopped to pick us up. My God, I thought, if I can sneak back into my room by midnight, I will survive.

We hit the Academy at 11:55 pm and I sprinted up the stairs and got to my door, my hand on the doorknob. The door was half way open when my good buddy Warren, the cadet in charge, found me.

Warren asked if I was authorized to be out of my room.

Now here is the grind, the moment of truth. I could have said yes, and stepped into my room, unscathed.

But I couldn't break the Academy honor code I believed in.

I couldn't lie.

I looked him in the eyes and said, "No, I'm not."

He looked sad because he knew the trouble I was in.

As Kelly remembered the story, "You were always a trouble maker, but I admire your adherence to the code."

"Thanks, Colonel, I wonder how much honor lurks around this enterprise."

"As much as you can stand, Lieutenant."

The thing is Kelly was not only ancient, he had a bunch of kids, and rumor had it: a family with a lot of money.

I emotionally threw up my hands at my fear of his doom and we kept drinking together.

A lot.

He could have stayed in his trailer with the other Majors and above, but he liked it in the crazy bar.

And so did I.

When he died, blown up by a faulty fuse on a bomb up north, it just increased the pain.

See, he didn't die because he was old or slow, or he clanked up.

He died by exploding, luckless fate.

I believe in fate, I hate fate and yet fate has taken care of me; spared me.

Sammy Martin thrice descends

#1

Sammy looks up and sees his parachute

he looks down through his feet at the south china sea

pumping his blood through wide open veins

he sees a raft dangling on its tether strung

from the seat pack so it floats and welcomes

airman landing in american controlled sea

#2

first time Sammy rolls downhill that day

sixty-degree dive bomb you see

seeking trucks hiding in green canopy while

trees spit out composite steel

spraying up hews of color

stay away! Sammy! stay away!

#3

forty-thousand pounds of shudder and fire

as Sammy prays for elemental water

he's from the southern carolina coast

and many a day did he chase the belles

from dance floor to convertible to sea shore

licking salt off willing skin

#4

the chopper hovered blowing foam on Sammy

his salt soaked eyes the harness coming down

Sammy hooked into the loop and second assent began

up Sammy! look at that wavering savior

its cord strung down umbilically pulling

wanting you inside sucking you up

#5

Sammy grasps at the birds entrance with a washed anxiety

he pulls and is pulled closer, closer

But his suit is soaked with war and sea

and his grip and his saviors grip cannot hold him

he falls away from agape rescue through prop wash

And for a third and last time descends

CHAPTER 22

Road Cutting Raga

The flight with the 72 big ones and the drinking session changed my relationship with Westerly. It was quieter, softer, and more tolerant. There was understanding. The war was completely bloody and completely hopeless. We had gotten ourselves into a bad one, and we both knew it.

In later flights, when we flew together we would try to get road cutting jobs. These required us to go to a remote road somewhere in the north or Laos, always in the mountains, and try to destroy a section of road or trail, usually at a cutback. It wasn't easy to do, but if you hit the thing just right, above the road, it caused a landslide, which probably took repair crews a day or two of work. To me that wasn't the point. The point was not to be dropping the fucking bombs on people.

A couple of those flights were almost pleasurable. We would just cook around the mountains looking for the right road, almost like high tech developers scouting for a site.

"Hey, that looks like a nice little road. How about some free earth moving?"

"What have you got in mind?" Westerly pulls the machine a little tighter.

"Why don't we knock out the road at that turn in anticipation of a nice cul-de-sac? Maybe Giap will want a summer home here, after he's done kicking our asses."

Hank hits it perfect. We pull out and roll over and watch the road slice away. It was a rare moment of dive-bombing tranquility; just us with the sliding mountain and tumbling dirt.

"We should do this everyday. Too bad they don't know you're finally figuring out this bombing thing, Major."

"Thanks. You think that'll keep them busy?"

Before I can answer, Two comes in the horn to tell Westerly he nailed it. It was starting to sound like a golf match.

As Westerly turns for Da Nang, I'm thinking this is the way wars should be fought. We blow up dirt and stone, they dig it out. Everyone makes money and no one gets hurt except the American people who still have to pay for it.

The end result would be the same. We pack up our toys and go home and they have better roads with which to build their country.

Uncle James – 1953

#1

"tell them the story, tell them what you did..."

my brother and I in the backseat

looking at our strange aunt

talk hard at james, her husband- mom's brother

only son of Rufus and Ethyl

town joke for his drinking

town joke for his stuttering

I loved him with my ten-year-old soul

I loved him for his mystery

I loved him for my absent father

#2

James drives on down highway 62 and

"they had me on the point in the Ardennes

hunting like I did back in the Illinois trees

weren't no 410 or twelve gauge though

it was a thompson they gave me, forty-five caliber

#3

"through a door in a forest hut I slammed

there in uniform was three german officers

one was a woman dressed in black holding a bottle of wine

the men were on either side- there was a big map on a table

I was strong and had the drop, had the drop

the men put their hands up... quick too

but the woman... bu... but the wo... woman

sh... she dropped the bottle and and went for her side arm"

#4

who knows my aunts purpose for pushing him on

for his silence then was enough even for a kid

'you killed em all didn't you?"

and he nods at her question... his rippled arm steering the chevy

I looked out the window

at dark fields and black unseen things

waiting patiently for me

CHAPTER 23

Khe Sahn Smoke Screen

In the beginning it was all the North's way. The weather, which even by Southeast Asian standards was horrible, precluded any kind of actual visual identification. Day after day it either rained or threatened, for that winter turned out to be one of the gloomiest on record.

Maybe Giap was a storm prognosticator. Certainly he had a plan.

The briefing on his latest move was a threat and a promise.

Some guy from Saigon is rattling along.

Actually he's parroting, pontificating the official crap he's been given. But here we go again.

"He's going to try a Dien Bien Phu type maneuver. Three confirmed divisions, maybe four, are being placed around a joint marine and South Vietnam outpost in the hilly country northwest of Da Nang. A place called Khe Sahn."

He points to a place on the map.

Yep, its northwest of here and it's hilly, alright.

I'm thinking that the old Dien Bien Phu-er has stepped in it this time.

Actually, it is not a place I'd seen much of. I'm getting close to 80 missions North and I'm wondering if this is going to be a risky deal that does nothing but lay my ass open to non-productive bullets. If it doesn't get me closer to leaving this A Shau Valley of Tears, it sucks.

Khe Sahn was a Marine outpost on a hill. There was an airstrip; big enough to land cargo ships like C-130s. Four engines and high-winged, the Hercules could land almost anywhere, and in marginal weather.

Trouble was fighters couldn't operate under these clouds. There was too little altitude.

So, I figured, as day after day we ran level radar guided bomb drops above the clouds, this is non-counting but possibly an ass saving filler. Maybe we were helping.

Trouble was the C-130s were getting absolutely hammered trying to resupply the poor bastards getting stuck down there. The North had the place zeroed with their artillery and the NVA anti-aircraft fire was withering.

Enter the same genius types who came up with the river mines. Another one of those fucks that came from some patriotic corporation.

"Gentlemen, this new smoke bomb is going to do the job. Here's what you do. Take F-4s down to hill level, one side of the runway."

This clown is from 3M, which as near as I can figure stands for Minnesota Murder and Mayhem, telling us all about it. I can see him now when he goes home.

"Yeah, honey, it was pretty hairy being that close to the enemy and everything but we all have to sacrifice and our men need those new smoke bombs bad. And you know what the boss said about the profit margin. I feel a little guilty saying it but we've never made more money and Mr. Jones said the bonus looks good this year."

I'd ten times rather drink with the average NVA grunt than pukes like this. They're always coming around, generally the PR types. Real friendly like, they have little idea of any reality that interests me.

I bet Napoleon's boys had the same problem.

"Monsieur le Captain, you must see the latest musket from Paris. Oui, it will solve your um, petit problem avec the Russians. Non, non, it will be impossible to accompany you to the front as you see I must go back immediately to zee company for more weapons development. Bon chance, Captain. Au Revoir."

So, back to the 20th century and the briefing.

"About a mile before you get to the runway, start releasing these smoke bombs. They will putt-putt off every ten seconds, causing a wall-like smoke curtain on either side of the approach to the runway. The C-130s will then fly down this corridor of smoke, shielded from the guns of the enemy. After all they can't hit what they can't see."

I feel extremely skeptical. I feel slightly sick. I feel completely alienated from another fucking scheme that puts our asses on the line.

On the other hand I feel some sympathy for the 130 drivers, who could use some help. And, we should be going fast enough to keep from…oh, hell, who knew?

As usual I'm on the first flight to try. This propensity to be on first missions has something to do with a cosmic drama deal, near as I can figure. Certainly it isn't about me being a first rate backseater. I'm literally sizzling to get out of this nightmare.

Maybe, I think as we walk out of the plane…wait, I'm diverted by a sweet stewardess looking down at us from one of the airliners.

"Hi," I wave. "Ask the Captain how much extra he made for landing here today. Will you please?" The lady smiles with a little anxiety tacked on.

Just then an airline clown with those cute hats they wear sticks his head around the stewardess. An actually really cool pilot guy…

I walk over to the base of their ramp, look up and start talking really nice to the guy.

"Gee, I hope it wasn't too bad for you coming in here and everything but I know you guys get an extra 500 bucks for landing at nasty old Da Nang. Gosh that's great. You know we fellow lovers of the sky also get extra pay. Yeah. We get 70 dollars a month. Every month too. Sometimes I feel guilty taking all that money, boy."

Westerly gets pissed.

"Will you quit with that freaking airline bashing? For Christ's sake, Oliver."

"But they make me sick, Maj. They…" I grab my stomach and pretend to get sick. The stewardesses look at me strangely.

"I know your problem. You think this will queer your chances with them."

Westerly shakes his head.

"What about yours?" he asks.

"I don't have time for them, Maj. What with drinking and jacking off twice a day. And then there is the intensive combat flight planning."

Westerly is laughing as we arrive at old 527 Delta. Looks okay on the preflight.

There's a weird ass contraption to hold the smoke bombs. But someone had to unload the smoke bombs. That's us. And someone is making a million on it. That's not us.

On the way to Khe Sahn, I ask Westerly,

"Think this will work?"

"Who knows? But it would be nice, and we will at least get to see the damn place."

I had just found out that Westerly had given me a bad OER.

I'm getting my ass hammered, we're all getting our asses hammered, and my frontseater is giving me bad ratings.

Meanwhile, you can bet some dipshit supply guy in Saigon is getting great ratings from his dipshit boss. Hey, Westerly. Who the fuck cares? The only rating I care about is the cosmic luck rating. Let that one be right and you can put me at the bottom of any and all anal theories on management and value.

Because no one is freer than someone who doesn't give a shit about the system they are in.

"Yeah," I mumble back to the helmet in front of me. "If we can get to the runway in one piece."

There's a broken cloud deck that Westerly, having put Two in trail, punches us through.

The usual green, contrasted with wisps of rain fog, beautiful really, it belies the hell 30 miles further west. We push on, about 1,500 feet above ground, trying to contact the big guys.

"Red flight, this is a big shaky one with two C-130s about 20 east of the drop. Over."

Westerly responds with our position and we smoke ass for the large guys. It's rare for us exotics to get anywhere near a prop bird, but then this is a rare treat. We're flopping and zooming around under the cloud deck, 40,000 NVA underneath us, all of whom have weapons that can bring us down. I'll tell you I'm so happy I could spit. We roll inverted and there they are, in all their camouflaged glory.

"Can you see the runway, should be 12 o'clock."

Westerly puts Two about 1,000 feet off our right wing.

"Roger, Shaky, we're starting in."

Small arms fire is impossible to see, but you can feel it. Westerly knows this and he pushes it up to about 500 knots. He isn't really happy about this going-straight-and-level shit either. The closer we get the more moonlike the terrain, for weeks of around-the-clock bombing had literally denuded the landscape. The US has killed everything but the enemy.

We get the release point and I'm watching the wingman. Out comes the smoke cans and it looks pretty good as things go off. And they do seem to be spreading a wall like a cloak of grey.

"Two, yours look good."

"Roger. Lead, yours too.

We're like two brides admiring our trains.

Then we're over the Khe Sahn runway.

Jesus.

Burnt out tanks and trucks. There was dusty red mud, a pockmarked runway, sandbags and actual rounds landing as we flew over.

I see no humans. Perhaps it's not healthy to be running around down there. Suddenly the C-130s are on the radio.

"Hey, this stuff is obscuring. The smoke is blowing all over… hell; we're flying blind here."

There's a pause as Westerly wrenches the beast back and forth, finally, we're back to my beloved jinking.

"Shaky One is pulling up, pulling up. Pull up Two!"

The smoke has blown over the flight path. Instead of two walls of cover it was like we laid a cloud down. We've created zero visibility. There we go again. God-like, we can make the weather.

The C-130s abandon the run. They can't see a damn thing.

Westerly is quiet for a while, and we get above the clouds and head for the base.

"Maybe we should drop the North Vietnamese girly magazines. While they're looking at them, our boys can sneak in. Huh, Major."

I always say Major while I'm wisecracking, figuring he won't get as pissed.

"The North doesn't have girly magazines, Oliver."

"I'd be glad to edit one for them. See it now. Wanted: armed, sexy girls of the North. Call Da Nang…"

"Shut up, Oliver."

I guess that Westerly still has a vestige of hope we are actually doing something. Later it was revealed that the C-130s waited for the smoke to clear and went in again. Seems they got hosed real good, as usual.

We never heard anymore about smoke walls. Guess they went the same place as the river mines and all the other great ideas our way of life provided for us.

This technological wonder we were in was being used like shit. These bodies we were given were being used to kill other bodies. All wonders, all miracles, all fucked up. A fighter plane as a metaphor sure had some juice.

Power, genius, and worthlessness.

CHAPTER 24

Circling, Circling, Circling

The NVA were screwed. Close air is about visibility, just ask the guys at the Battle of the Bulge, when the weather also precluded air support. And now suddenly we had it at Khe Sahn-good visibility I mean. We were like angry bees, buzzing around and anxious to bite.

Khe Sahn had cleared. After weeks of crappy obscuring clouds the place broke out. Sun hit the hills and we hit where the sun did shine.

That freakin' battle was over the moment we could see the ground. As ambivalent as I was about the war the warrior in me was aroused, especially as we were helping our own.

Combat and universality don't usually march together. You have to believe your side has more merit than the other and that day I did.

The NVA had been digging trenches up the side of the main hill zigzag style like they used at Dien Ben Phu except here the US had countless fighters within 100 miles. We swarmed and that bitch of a fight was essentially over...but of course the ramifications back home continued.

After we expended everything we got a radio call.

Next thing we're cranking four to five g turns around this hilltop near Khe Sahn for ten minutes while below us, 40,000 or so North Vietnamese are trying their best to kill us and that's what we want.

Why?

Because some poor bastard got his spinal cord slashed by flashes of metal and there's a hovering helicopter that I can see occasionally as we spin around and around; and if the NVA is shooting at us, they won't shoot at the rescue guys, and maybe, the thinking goes, the NVA gunners won't pop us 'cause we're SO FAST. But I can't help thinking, please get his ass off that hill so we can blow back to Da Nang and maybe later give ourselves a congratulatory drink or something.

Finally, the radio releases us, tells us the chopper's clear. It's amazing how powerful human voices on a Marconi can be, and praise be all that power when it tells you to go home, short though that relief can be.

Never found out about the guy on that hill - never do.

But I got a DFC for that mission and maybe that's ok; maybe we saved someone; maybe he had some kind of life.

CHAPTER 25

Hunger Grows

So when Faust sees me getting counters out of those close air support missions north of the base, he starts putting me on the most southerly of the in-country rides. He gets me on the first one-no chance to convert, but on the second I drew this new dude who had the look of a willing pupil. I had ninety north and the hunger grew. I wanted to eat the cadaver of my tour, all 100 bones, and belch all the way to the States.

I broach the subject slowly.

"You know some of these things in-country are over real quick."

"Yeah, that sounds okay to me Oliver."

"It can be more than okay, if you're interested."

He is and we get a quick pass and a dismissal of ordinance and we flip another one.

That night the Flippers Club has a meeting. Montague is laughing at me because he thinks I'm dicked on my next days scheduled ride and that I'm in for a real slowdown in counters.

It's a radar guided bomb run in Laos.

"You've made the most enemies, Oliver. And you're ten, fifteen ahead of everybody else that got here in August."

"Fuck you guys. I'm going to convert that piece of shit. I'm not stopping at 91."

Bets were made.

And I knew there was a shot because of the good major Prentice. Me, him, and Phantom makes three.

The problem here was all the bombs were 750s, and the things were to be dropped on one pass, flying level at altitude. It was the safest of missions, except for the fact that carrying bombs over a combat zone ain't ever safe.

We were Lead, the weather sucked and Laos awaited our offerings with a gloomy resignation. Laos always depressed me. How did they get almost as many explosions, probably more per capita, as the real litigants here?

I was here to lessen that injustice.

Ah, the research, the leaning forward to peer at 100 circuit breakers and the Eureka! when the correct one shows itself. There in the middle of the fourth row sticking its little black head up was number 92. Salvation is where you find it. The universe helps those that can pull things at the right moment.

"Turn left two degrees, climb twenty feet. Hold heading and altitude. Five, four, three, two, one…Pickle."

The ground control radar guy sounds bored.

The rumbling release was so familiar but so different this time. Normally when the beast let go of her horrors I was relieved. This time at the half way point, NOW! I pulled the button and all fell silent for a second. Then, unexpectedly the old major goes ape shit.

"What the fuck! They quit releasing. Goddammit. I had a feeling something was going to…Shit now we gotta carry these things."

Like a good therapist I wait for the right moment, the pause that allows an interjection.

"Uh, Major why don't you let me call Hillsbourgh and get clearance into PAC One for disposal. And recycle all your switches. I'll check the circuit breakers. Hey, look at that. I got one out. Let's see…it's the internal bomb…yeah, it reset sir. That should work. Some kind of electrical glitch, hopefully."

The wingman pulls up close, empty of his load. Those two over there owe me but they'll never know why. They're about to get the easiest flip of the tour and they don't even know the real benefactor. Just like those guys in congress, it's the old timers that show the newly elected the best way to steal. I am chairman of the flipping committee, and my vote rules. Follow me for payday, boys; you don't even have to understand.

Payday for the dedicated flipper, but what about the jungle below? What fateful cosmic chance was altered, what explosion transposed, what living being spared, what innocence vaporized?

Was there some poor Laotian huddling against the steel rain when it suddenly stopped just short of his guts? Was there some poor Vietnamese suddenly dismembered because some alienated foreigner allowed the shit to come down on what he hoped was nobody just so he could finish the nightmare quicker?

There was on the backseat control stick a bomb release button. I never pushed it in 160 missions. I never discussed this with anybody until one drunken night it was blurted out to Kromer. He said nothing, staring at me without emotion for a moment then he nodded and looked away. And I knew it didn't mean much, it didn't console.

When the scheduling Guru sees this he goes me one better, he thinks. He basically shuts me down. No real flying, just test hops and ferrying stuff to Formosa for repairs. When I get back from the Island of our allies, it's off to the records room for me.

Assault on the numbers. No moneychanger, no bean counter, no forger went to the books with more passion.

Every mission was recorded on strange wide computer read outs, tended by a couple of bored, safe airmen. Surprised to see me they lay scrolls in front of me and stand off, curious.

"Just wanted to make sure these babies are right. Got my own copy of missions and you know how things could have been…"

That was a lie, actually. I had not a single damn thing written down anywhere.

"Yes, sir, Lieutenant. You let us know if we can correct anything."

I was surprised at the guy's tone and look up into a smiling face. Cool! He's got as long as possible hair and a peace symbol ring and he's smiling the intelligent rebellious enlisted man smile. This cat has figured the game and thinks it's funny, and he's rebellious as hell.

"Here's one in September that was a missed counter, and here's another one and here's one last month I think…"

"Better safe than sorry, sir. I'll just make a mark. Any others?"

I walk out with four more and the big 95 has been breached. Yeah, verily, even though I walk through the valley of stop the mad flipper, I shall convert forever. You fuckers can't stop me. I am the mad bomber, redistributor of death, rethrower of the American flowers of evil. Who will be the next bridesmaid to catch one of my bouquets?

No one I hope. I sometimes lay awake imagining bombs landing in empty jungle, which is of course impossible. Nothing is less empty than a jungle. I guess it's people I don't want to kill, though all the critters we blew up…

Just to make sure the next stop is to Hank's office in the maintenance hangar.

"What's happening, Oliver? I haven't seen you for awhile. Are the frontseaters performing to your high standards?"

"Actually, Major, I was hoping we could fly together some the next week or so. Kind of for old times sake. You see, I have 95 north and it's going to be over soon and…"

"You have how many?"

"95, sir."

"Jesus, Oliver that's impossible. We've only been here seven months. Christ I only have 50 something. How the hell did you do...wait a minute...I don't think I want to know."

"Well after the crash, I went into maximum flying mode. You know that we're supposed to fly a lot to get over traumas like frontseaters that can't land in adverse conditions."

Westerly grins and asks.

"Do you think I could have made that landing?"

"Hell yes and so could I"

Westerly looks closely and smiles.

"What's the real reason that you came in here?"

"I want to finish and I know they'll schedule us for counters if you'll commit to fly with me for a week. It won't hurt your total either, sir. And you've gotten pretty good and you don't scare the shit out of me like most of the rest. This whole damn thing would have been a lot easier if they hadn't made you maintenance officer. And forced me into gypsy backseater. Fodder for the masses. That's me, Major."

I smiled and Westerly looked back for a second like an older brother, and gave me the wistful stare.

"I'll never get out of here early. They need me to run this thing. But even though you're as crazy as a loon or maybe because you're as crazy as a fox...tell them to schedule us. Now get lost, some of us are trying to run a war."

And some of us, old West Pointer, are trying to run away from the fucker, only to come back. But you know that, don't you, don't you, don't you???

CHAPTER 26

The Last Ride: Not with a Whimper but a Bang

99, what a number. It has symmetry and hidden meaning. It's the last of the double digits and the portal to completion.

100 percent is the whole of anything and 100 missions North is the whole of this stinkin' tour. And I wonder if the Air Force had a romantic heart when they picked it. Why not 98 or 105?

Whatever.

After converting number 99, I didn't anticipate any help from Faust. But, amazingly he put me on a night bombing run up North.

He had had enough, me thinks. And he wanted me gone.

Me too.

It wasn't anything spectacular that last ride, just more destruction or at least explosions on some beach near Dong Hoi.

Westerly flew it with me, then shook my hand and said, "Good luck upgrading. I hope to hell you're a better frontseater than back."

"How could I not, Major? You may still be here when I get back. Maybe I could fly your wing."

"Maybe in the States if you don't get court-martialed, Oliver. So long."

Portentous bastard, that Westerly, as I almost did get thrown out but had to settle for an Article 15. It's one stop short of court-martial, but one step beyond what any other officer I ever knew received.

Rites Rites Rites

#1

in other saner towns there were rites of return

there were rituals and fine madnessess

there was weeping and stories and laments and regrets and love

and

respect and respect and respect

there were fires that burned late and wine and mushrooms and

pot and other ways to

go to the other mind and fuse your own forgiveness

in other saner towns

CHAPTER 27

Training and Alienation

I staggered home, 160 missions in 210 days.

Idiots and idiot savants, bureaucrats, cargo pilot poseurs, and the occasional true rocker had all shown me their juice or lack thereof. People had died in mass numbers among us, in spite of us, because of us, below us and above us. They'd even been saved because of us. Of course this probably meant somebody else got fried.

Now, with my emotional center shattered but with my warrior face seething to control the fight I go back to the US wrenched with a similar dichotomy. It's the spring of 1968. Landing in San Francisco, I took a cab to the city and right at Candlestick Park we blow a tire, and as the cabby starts to change it, I stepped outside. We were on the side of the freeway and cars were flying by. Close. I couldn't believe what I felt. It was fucking scary to watch this guy squatting casually what seemed to me to be within a few feet of instant death. Ironically, at Da Nang everything like traffic was orderly and safe. This seemed insane, unreal-America to an outsider.

They gave the backseaters a choice of any airplane. How about instructing in some dump in Texas, or sit Strangelove-like on nukes in some other dump in Kansas, or fly bus-like cargo jobs that stayed in the air as long as a summer's day. Or fly air defense where you flew above any hope of tasting the borderline of earth and sky. For what is atmosphere but the contrasts of taste and motif? In other words, who the fuck wants to be at high altitude, probably in weather?

Screw all that isn't the monster. I want the monster, I need the monster. F-4. Four times fucked I was for loving her.

"Fine," they said. "Only one thing. If we give you the beast, there's one little thing. You have to control her, consort with her back where she most belongs. You have to come back to…IT. It still grows and it's American minions that need beast masters. You have been bloodied and you have been bent, now come, come back to the feeding ground." I knew it was beyond bullshit, but I couldn't help myself. Like the guy in 'Of Human Bondage,' the whore had me.

The training for upgrading was at McDill Air Force Base. Its runway was 13,500 feet long and 500 feet wide, maybe the biggest in the world.

It was my second time at McDill. Hank and I had trained there. On our first pre-Vietnam mission to the bombing range in the bowels of Florida, one of the other planes called a fire light. As we approached from the rear it was obvious this warning light had it right. The whole damn right interior wing was burning.

It was cool.

Hank screamed for them to eject, as they did because the manual on fires was definitive, if it's burning, blow the fuck out of there-NOW! By chance they must have pulled the handles at the same time because the canopies blew off exactly together, and the seats came out together, and the chutes opened together, and the crew floated down together, talking to each other all the way.

We rolled over and followed the thing to its grave.

Inverted, we floated downward with the abandoned beast. It seemed stable at first as if the humans weren't necessary, like a wild stallion that a cowboy jumps off. Then, in a last signal of her sudden need, she rolled inverted and hit, the empty cockpits seemingly the first to explode.

The backseater had a compression fracture of his spine, the first of many cracked spines acquired from ejecting.

Why?

The seat was made by Martin Baker, an English firm specializing in shit-ball designs. Typically British, it had Rube Goldberg concepts of never using one part when four would do. The rumor was that the US bought the thing to throw some business to that benighted little island. The back fractures were especially fucked during the war when some poor bastard, and a bunch of guys from my Wing fit this description, found himself running and hiding in North Vietnam, or Laos with a wrenching pain in his back. The phenomenon led the British to send to Da Nang the most aviator-like looking dude I ever laid my pissed off eyes on to calm our asses down. Huge handle bar mustache and a big grin, charming as hell. My first inclination was to drop the fucker in his tracks until it dawned on me he was an entertainer, a hired monkey as it were. It was the PT Barnums of this fucking circus I wanted to hate. And no, they weren't anywhere near our little sideshow. They were running all over Washington selling shit and blowing smoke up the ass of the Congressmen and stuffing money down their mouths.

"Want you blokes to know my great pleasure in being here at the front. My company will spare nothing in getting to the problem."

The problem, pal, is way beyond your Limey ass.

Back to McDill, I don't know what I expected at the upgrading class. 20 frontseaters and their backseat counterparts. By this time the Air Force was putting more navigators in the rear, though there were still some pilots. It seemed to be more of a mix for the fronts. There were a few old fighter pilots that got shaken out of some other deal, and a lot of guys that had previously been wannabes. The thing that surprised me was the instructors. Some hadn't even been to Nam yet. Some had. They were also a mixture of training command types, transplanted F-100 instructors and a few real F-4 heads.

The funny thing was the disdain I sensed towards me from some of the war veterans. There was some blatant whispering behind my back and I couldn't figure it. Finally, I got to know one of the decent instructors and described both my tour and my confusion as to some people's attitude about me. He explained that some of them thought I hadn't earned my upgrade slot because my missions didn't include Hanoi.

"You should tell some of these guys exactly what Da Nang was all about, Oliver."

"Do me a favor and let me do it my own way."

I had no intention of telling the butt holes anything at all and I never did. Fuck 'em. I wanted to be misunderstood.

But the guy that everyone seemed to revere was a slight, balding, unassuming guy named Mike something. It seemed that he had fought four Mig's by himself. And not only shot one down, but damaged another before exiting southward. He was resigning his commission in order to fly airlines. I was horrified that someone that good was leaving to fly a bus. When I asked how he could do such a thing it was explained that he wasn't a college grad and therefore stood no chance of 'real' advancement. So fucking what that he wasn't a grad of some dink college? That was more of that bullshit bomber crap. A system of advancement based on political, conformist factors, not the skill in the job you really did.

So, they gave me a backseater pilot who I resolved to honor for his guts and his screwed up deal. His name was Tony and he was a cliché with bells. A tough New Jersey Italian who listened when I talked and who had experience with fist fighting, closer than you'd think to an applicable skill.

"I'll teach you everything I can to help you survive the big show, Tony. Backseat pilots are a joke but there are many things you can do with your personality and your voice to increase chances of making it back to the family."

"Thanks."

"It's fucked, this thing, Tony But the ride...god...the ride. In its fury...there's nothing...Uh, just wait until dogfighting practice. I think there's a way to crew...to coordinate our efforts. Of course you'll be under six g's and do not get caught leaning forward when I lay on the beef or you won't get upright for awhile. It hurts."

"Can't wait, Ron."

"I've got to check out with a guy named Green. Buddy Green. After that it's my machine and then we can train this deal right."

Yes, the American penchant for teaching.

We will teach the VC not to fuck with us, or the millions in jail or the Native Americans.

In an empire, teaching is a euphemism for torture and pain.

All I've learned is to resist any more 'knowledge.' I don't want to be taught anything more by the bastards that started all this shit.

It may take me lifetimes, centuries to undo what has already been jammed down my throat.

CHAPTER 28

Me and Tony Fight Buddy

Me and Tony fight Buddy to a bloody draw. Almost.

Buddy's pre-brief was simple. We go up in a Two ship and head to the Gulf of Mexico where there's an area to fight in; it's a ring, a circle, or a cylinder from fifty thousand feet to the deck, which was water. The day before, one of the instructors, a guy named Eddings, had been up dog-fighting his student, Smith, when Eddings bent it wrong and she spun. When the F-4 spun, it was highly unlikely that it could be saved. All three axes of control are lost in a full-blown spin, kind of like a 40,000 pound leaf falling. The best you could do was press the rudder opposite the direction of the spin, wait for a full turn, pop the drag chute (which usually shredded off), and slam the stick forward. This would sometimes bring the flight controls back into effectiveness, but not often. Spins were mysterious, violent, whacky non-sequiturs. Eddings fought and pushed and slammed the machine but he couldn't get it out by 10,000 so he and the backseater punched out. This instructor was a big, unusually overweight guy. Smith, in the other bird circled Eddings, watching as he tried to get in the raft. The backseater easily got into his, of course.

Later in the bar, Smith says,

"It was worth two and a half million in aircraft just to see Eddings try to get into his raft."

Anyway, this is the way we practice dogfighting. We split off 45 degrees from each other, go out 20 to 25 miles and turn in.

May the best man win.

When the turn was called, Buddy was out of sight, so I shoved the throttle to 100 percent, then a little to the left and all the way to the wall, which is full afterburner, unloaded a hair, to .7 g which is the maximum acceleration curve and headed right at him, or where I thought he was. He did the exact same thing. We were 1.7 mach when Tony calls him at 10 o'clock level.

I hammered the fucking beast; 6 g's pulling her like a bitch in heat. Improbable shit. The goddamn species has evolved this far in mechanical competence and insanity and they have built incredible equipment to play stupid fucking games and I'm going for it.

I HAVE NO FUCKING CHOICE! I MUST! I MUST! I MUST!

I jammed my feet on the rudders to turn because under heavy g's the F-4's ailerons are worthless. In fact they were deadly. They couldn't be used at all or the thing would go into an opposite turn for complicated aerodynamic reasons. It was spooky turning with rudder, the instinct screamed to push the stick in the direction desired. In dogfighting the eccentric F-4, you had to hold the stick straight as you pulled, pulled, pulled it back, slamming the rudder in the desired direction.

We cross Buddy and I jam the other rudder just as Tony screams,

"Reverse!"

It's amazing to have a voice in your ear, speaking what you're doing at the exact same time you're doing it. It's astoundingly reinforcing.

Something wants me to do this well, and watches this fight, something that needs this as much as I.

We stayed even with Buddy. We bent it as hard as he did.

Twice we got it down to ten thousand and called it off, with no advantage either way.

The third time looked the same…until Buddy started to slide back and low in my vision, I mean I'm looking down left and there's Buddy maybe a couple of thousand below and at 7 o'clock. I'm freaked and confused. How the fuck…?

Buddy calls for Fox Two, which means he's fired a theoretical missile that might have gotten our asses.

We come home and debrief.

I'm impressed.

And I want you to know what the hell he did on the third encounter.

"You fought great, Oliver. Good offense and defense."

"Okay, but about the third time when you got behind me…"

Buddy shows a thin grin.

"That's my secret, sorry."

And the guy means it. I can see it in his eyes; he ain't telling me his little freakin' trick.

He ain't telling me something that can save my life!

Hell, I might have been on his wing someday and…aw, the hell with that. It's that bizarre and inchoate.

One day chasing Buddy

he tried to go straight up

I took the bait

And followed

but it could not last

and when he fell back, two pipes growing

in my windscreen

frothing white smoke

I kicked out

for fear of merger

CHAPTER 29

Range Wars

They didn't send me back to Vietnam. The two squadrons in my wing from Homestead Air Force Base were sent to Kunsan Air Force Base, South Korea instead.

Southwest coast, beautiful, it was nothing like the images in my mind of the northern Chosin Reservoir: winter, snow, Korean War nightmare thing.

My dad had barely escaped the Chinese, when he was on the last C-47 out of a forward base, looking down at the swarming Chinese army coming through the perimeter. I have always had a thing for Korea.

This was a resort area and proved to be great flying.

The gunnery range was on an island in a river. Very cool.

I got hot on the gunnery range there and led my squadron in range scores. Until one day on a rocket pass, I had trouble getting my pipper on the target and I pressed lower and lower. Suddenly an alarm went off in my head. I was way too low and in trouble. I knew I couldn't just snatch big g's on the sucker because that would make me mush in a pancake aerial skid. So,

I pulled the nose up firmly until the nose was just above the horizon, lit afterburner, and prayed.

This is how close it was. The pilot on the ground observing told me later,

"I couldn't even foul you for being too low, I was too scared. You actually blew dirt up with the burners. Maybe ten feet is all you had left."

The two squadrons we replaced were going to Vietnam.

I ran into an AFA classmate Tommy Rodriguez, who loved Korea, and told me he did not want to leave.

"Cool, Tommy, good luck in Nam."

Tommy had a great singing voice and could have been a pro. One time at the Academy, a singing group called Fred Warring and the Pennsylvanians came through for a concert, heard Tommy sing, and tried to get him to resign from school and join them.

But Tommy wanted to fly.

A couple months later, we heard Tommy was hit in the head by a single bullet through the front cockpit and killed.

I never said good-bye to Tommy but I'll say it now.

You were a good one, Tommy.

Late in my dance with the death wagon, back in the States, I feared no one at the gunnery range. No one. It was my thing, my outlet, it was measured and chronicled, thus no argument. To me it was a way to make the game meaningful. The scores were the scores. No one could argue with them, or so I thought. I was kicking ass.

Enter the Wing Commander one day. He appears at our squadron with two of his toadie frontseaters. They needed another guy to fill out the four ships and maybe because of my reputation as a top gunner they put me in the flight.

It was a standard ride. Three dive bombs, three rockets, then down to the deck for three skip bombs and then the piece de resistance-strafe. Ah, strafe, the most satisfying of all range events. It was clearly my favorite. You came honking in low, get the pipper on the target panel and squeeze off, ideally, twenty or thirty rounds and get out before the foul line at or above 100 feet.

That was a game worth the price.

The Gatling gun shot 4,000 or 6,000 rounds a minute, 100 rounds a second at the faster setting, which I used. My reasoning was when the pipper was on the panel I wanted to smoke the fucker quick. So, we are talking one quarter second bursts or less, if you wanted to be a real player. Now that I think about it, isn't that the duration of an orgasmic squirt-penis or 20 mm-what the hell, they be fun. One of my earlier squadron commanders used to insist we shoot 100 rounds per range ride. This meant 33 per pass. I hated this. It was forcing me into too long of a burst, longer bursts were harder to keep on the target. One night in a bar in Korea I had it out with him. I was in tight competition with another young frontseater from the other squadron for Wing Top Gun, and their commander didn't insist on the 100 round rule.

"Are you telling me it will really help you beat that little twerp, Oliver?"

"You just watch, colonel."

"Okay, no minimum number."

Suddenly I was a surfer at Maverick's, a skier at Alta, a climber at K-2.

The next ride was one of my favorite moments in six and a half years.

I fired 67 rounds in three passes. When the scores came in I had 67 hits, a rare 100 percent strafe.

Back to the ol' Wing Commander at Homestead Air Force Base. I always figured he might be a blowhard and a rounder. The other two frontseaters were there slumming with the old man, typical in their smarmy mediocrity. I figured them for an easy win but didn't know for sure about the big guy; sometimes the old timers could still fly.

So the mission goes off. Garcia proves himself to be a lousy Lead. This is a subtle thing, leading other fighters, even in peacetime conditions. You've got to think ahead, you've got to be smooth, and hopefully come up with something interesting to do on the way to and from the range. I liked swooping down on trucks on the highway or weaving two ships back and forth across the other two ships, making neat patterns.

Something.

Garcia just drives us up to central Florida with no imagination. But that's alright; I just want my passes. When we got to the range the first thing is to make a fly by over the range just to get a feel for the winds and so the range officer could take a look at the flight. This is also where I used my secret trimming technique. Normally in the F-4, or any airplane, a pilot was trimming all the time; the trim was used to keep the airframe in perfect flying form. Essentially it was controlling small surface changes that we did with our right thumb on a little round knob on the stick.

On the range I trimmed on the first pass to 450 knots, which was the desired release speed for all four events. Then I never trimmed again the entire 12 runs. This was a very difficult thing; the old right thumb itched to do its thing on the trim button especially when pulling off a pass and getting back up to altitude. When the monster bleeds off airspeed it flies much different. It felt like hell, at say 300 knots, to horse it around the pattern out of trim. But for me, the point was to get to the release point on a bomb or rocket pass and just let off on the stick and know it was in perfect trim at 450 knots.

On the bomb runs, we rolled in at 6,000 feet. The trick here was to realize that even though the monster weighed 40,000 pounds you could still feel the wind moving it. I liked to roll inverted, then pull the nose down to 45 degrees, detecting by the beast's drift, if the announced wind seemed accurate. Much was intuitive about all this…

Hey!!! Wait a minute.

I mean here was this wonderful competition, kind of three-dimensional dart throwing at 500 mph and no one got hurt. I got to play with the damn thing. It was cool and I was a stoner kicking ass. This was one of the ways of dealing with the war and the fact it would always be there, in me a very gut checking, tearful sense.

It was like the old warrior plot where the cat gets beat up, goes back and becomes a master then goes back and kicks…you know.

Anyway we get back to the squadron after the ride.

Garcia speaks,

"I don't care about my bombs, rockets and skip bomb much, because I nailed strafe."

The toadies smile.

He couldn't care about the bombs and rockets and skip much because the scores were called on the range and his shit stunk.

Then the strafe scores come in from the range.

One-21 (Garcia).

Two-78 (me).

Three-25

Four-31.

I waited for the Colonel to finally show some class and just dismiss the fight so I can jump in my VW bus, roll a big joint and go play with DeeDee, my sweet girlfriend.

But no.

Garcia speaks.

"I think there was a mistake. I must have shot at the number Two panel on one pass."

The toadies turn to look at me.

One of them says,

"I've got an idea Colonel. Why don't you combine your score with number two, that's you Oliver, and divide the total by two? You both would have a nice score."

The Colonel loves it.

"Good idea, good idea."

There's a pause occasioned by absolutely no response from me. I figured if they thought about it a minute they would realize the bullshit quality of the idea.

But, noooo. The brown-noser finally looks at me.

"How about it, Captain?"

All I could think about was the real fighter pilots, living and dead. How they would rather die than sell out on either end of this horseshit and they were somewhere watching.

"A score's a score, Captain."

I saved the old man's face a little by addressing the underling.

"I smoked my panel."

The Colonel looks at me like I was a bad dinner. I smiled back at him like he was a watered down drink.

On crashing a Beechcraft Bonanza alone

the runway was right over there

a little thing

it received little things

like the 1949 machine I had taken off

after taking my self off the night before

sweating and aching

from boozy cocaine poisoning

the flight was to be contrite proof

that I was ok

that I could do both

that there was meaning left in mechanical lift

but aaah

the little bird gave up her electricity

and her nose wheel landing gear

unseeable through bloodstained eyes

rolled up into her body

and I was back in Vietnam

skidding skidding skidding

CHAPTER 30

Bach's Greatest Fallacy

Richard Bach's 'Night Flight,' is a paean to peacetime fighter flying.

Bach's admiration for true aviators is heart felt and his own career is second to few. Still, there is in Bach's book, "A Gift's Wings", the biggest crock of crap about fighter flying I have ever read. This does not mean that it isn't a widely held crock of crap.

Here's the deal.

Bach's flying Lead ship in an F-100. On his Wing his buddy Bo Beavens is in another F-100.

They were at a few hundred feet and Bach gets distracted in the cockpit. Something is broken and he's resetting a circuit breaker.

As Bach tells it,

"Suddenly, the Bo man calls in a question, and I quote,

'Do you plan on flying into this mountain?'

"I jerked my head up, startled, and there angled in front of us was a rugged little mountain, all brown rock and sand and tumbleweed, tilting, flying toward us at something over three hundred knots an hour. Beavens said nothing more. He didn't loosen his formation or move to break away. He spoke in the way he flew his airplane…if you choose to fly straight ahead, there will be not one hole in the rock but two."

Hello, Mister Bach. That's totally God damn dumb. If I'm on your Wing and you don't respond I after burner up to get your scattered attention. If you don't respond, it's bye-bye baby, because I'm not flying into a mountain because of your dumb ass.

Near the end of my Phantom days I was on the wing landing in night weather at our base in Homestead, Florida. The Lead was a good cat named Joe Fratelli. As we started descending on final, the weather got worse. I pulled in closer to Joe's right wing, the blinking red light inches from my canopy. It got bumpier.

Now there is this code so well delineated by Bach. YOU HAVE TO STAY ON THIS WING EVEN IF IT MIGHT KILL YOU AND YOUR BACKSEATER. IT IS JUST THE WAY IT IS.

I said fuck the code, radioed Joe that I was disengaging and slid back and out a little. I called up approach, did 360-degree level turn on the instruments. GCA picked me up and brought me in for a safe landing.

I waited for the encounter with Joe in the parking area. As I got out of the cockpit he was standing there with concern on his handsome face.

"What happened?"

"It just wasn't worth the effort, Joe. Fuck it. It was safer to come around on my own."

Now Joe respected my ability and he looked at me very kindly and said,

"That's pretty smart. I was just worried it was something I did wrong as Lead."

"No, Joe you were fine. I just didn't feel like coming. That's all."

CHAPTER 31

Billy's Story

His great bad luck was to draw the lead cowboy for his frontseater. One Major Luke Grandee, a fighter weapons school graduate and first rider on many a strange trail.

The hierarchy considered Grandee to be the stud of studs.

Impossible mission? Give it to Grandee and Parris.

Why not?

They probably had the best chance. And if they did not make it, it was still the defendable position.

There were careers to think about, after all.

So classified were these missions that no one outside of a very few "need to know" ever heard directly of these things.

Billy looks at me and starts,

"Grandee and I had already flown some serious shit together…."

Billy then looks at me, smiling,

"Not that you and everyone else didn't as well."

I had heard rumors, vague bar rumblings about very hairy, one-ship operations. But I did not give it much thought and I did not know it was Billy.

"The job wasn't destruction at all. It was the rarest of all things for a fighter, Oliver."

Billy is earnest, tragically serious.

He was, then, to me the epitome of a subgod caught in a human dilemma. He had seen the abyss and I was one of the few he could talk to about it.

"I planned it for three days. They tried to write a simulator program to help me with the radar mapping. It didn't do much good. You know simulators."

Yeah, I think I know, Will.

I know the real thing is always murkier and harder to read than a copy. That goes for flight simulators and that goes for people."

Will continues,

"We took off at two-thirty in the morning. The only thing we carried other than standard tip tanks were two canisters, one under each wing."

I interrupt.

"I thought we were hunter killers. Where the hell were you guys…?

"Listen, man, this is ironic."

Will stares out of the window at our fine-tuned lawn.

"We were on a supply mission. Yeah, our job was to deliver these cans to a valley north of Hanoi, in the pitch black. We had to go to northern Laos, refuel, and then go into Northern Vietnam, alone, for the mission."

I stop to think about just that part of the flight.

They were alone. Hell…normally we hunted in packs of at least two. It wasn't natural to be up there at all, but especially by your lonesome. If you went down with a running mate at least there was a chance they could start a rescue, spot you, and tell someone something.

Alone? Nada, baby, nada.

Second, they night refueled. Let me tell you something about night refueling.

Sometimes it was nice, if the weather was good. Smooth, orderly, beautifully timed dance of connection. Even then the wolf in me, the primitive, would feel...this could not be happening. This is impossible, hurtling through space, intricately connected to a huge tanker. Exchanging fluids, the male member of the tanker engorges the temporarily passive F-4 beast then disengages...without even a kiss.

You fall off, down into the depths of post-coital apprehension. The tanker recedes like a departing lover and you are alone again.

"Luke and I wanted decent weather but we didn't get it. We immediately went down to fly just above the mountains in Western North Vietnam, and I started the mission radar profile."

Billy looks at me and answers my unasked question.

"They fine-tuned the ground mapping on the bird we flew."

I say,

"The radar sucks in that mode, and we all know it."

I hated even turning that damn function on. The radar necessitated leaning way forward into the screen to see anything. The only time I ever got airsick was trying to read that piece of shit on low level training runs.

Further, the ground-mapping mode was a secondary consideration on the F-4.

The primary job, originally, was fleet defense or intercepting hostiles trying to do the Okinawa shuffle, or the Kamikaze boogies on those overpriced Navy carriers. The air-to-air radar function was effective, allowing the backseater to pick up enemy aircraft at long range, under the optimum conditions of being over water.

Now here is Billy being asked to use this primitive feature to go north under literally near impossible conditions. The penalty under the slightest error would be death on the side of a misread mountain.

Period.

In fact, had this insanity been demanded of me, I would have refused.

Despite the code, despite the ostracism, despite my own self-hatred, I was not good enough, brave enough for that one.

"We ran along to a point 50 miles west of Hanoi, and then we had to drop into the clouds. I had a mountaintop on the radar, so Luke and I knew where we punched through. But from then on, it was ejection seat of the pants flying."

"What in the hell was in those canisters, Will? What was worth that? What?"

He just looked at me, bashfully.

"Ron, we didn't know. We didn't even fucking know what they contained, or who they were for, or who the hell was down there. Man, it was black…those clouds. I was looking at the scope, but I could feel the dark. It was palpable. We didn't talk much, the only light was the turned down cockpit instruments."

"What about the winds? Even if you guys flew the profile perfectly…the bird could have been blown off course."

"Yeah, and we couldn't call Hanoi to get the latest weather. Then it got bumpy and the sheet lightening started. Waves of ridiculous flashes, hellish black, then more flashes."

Will takes another slug.

"Sometimes I think I can read it and sometimes…"

He shakes his head.

"It was basically a crap shoot for our lives with special effects. Did you ever see St. Elmo's Fire glowing down the wing?"

Yeah, Will, I saw the electric blue juice of the skyvoltage god painting our canopy with movable art. I saw. Looked like day glow water rolling down the Plexiglas. I sometimes thought if I could have reached through and FELT IT, maybe it would have been mine. Instead I crouched against another mystery, looking up in fearful awe. Of course…electrical disturbances around live bombs might have something to do with it.

I smiled at him and asked,

"You know that winter was the stormiest in decades, man? Wild elephantine clouds packed with electric waves and sound waves that surfed the sheets of water and wiped themselves out on the ground."

We started laughing.

"Poet."

Billy salutes. Then continues.

"We had to thread a needle and the lower we went the harder it got. I tried to figure the elevations, based on the time, distance and the little I could discern from the screen. There were minutes during which we could have died at any second. Interminable sections, then when we were still there, I would know we'd made it to another ridgeline. 5,000 then 4,000…I'd give Luke the headings, he'd follow them. It was one of those reversals of roles where both our asses were in my hands, not the frontseater."

"We couldn't make a mistake in any direction, and we had to find the right damn spot in the black. And we had to be back on the deck when we got there."

The irony of the mission, I realize now, was that the F-4 in a fluid environment, operated by someone who knew what he was doing, had a chance in even incredibly hostile conditions.

This mission took away the inherent advantages of the F-4 from Will and Luke. They had to thread a needle, go through a narrow tunnel of space to a specific point. No jinking, no dodging, nothing but grinding terror.

"Lower, then level, then lower, then level. Time and distance, that's all we really had and in a funny way that is all we needed."

Billy looks at me and smiles, his soul glistening through his eyes.

"We hit the valley and we got in. Suddenly I knew we could dive down. He shoved it over and we came out of the clouds and there were a few lights. LIGHTS…they were beautiful.

"I remember saying,

'Two minutes hold the heading and hold 1,500 feet.'

"Then the place went off. Everywhere. Fucking streams of guns. Just full out streamers all over the place. Below us, above us, around, all I could think was where the hell did they all come from?

"It was the only time on the whole tour that I saw no way out. I felt us get hit, and moved around, shuddering. All I could think was what the fuck? Then it was quiet and we were through. Somehow. I hadn't said a thing. It was too violent, too fast."

"I remember Luke saying,

'You all right?'

"And I said,

'Yeah! Did we get hit?'

"And he said,

'I think so and how long until we drop?'

"And I said,

'A minute, hold the heading.'

"And we rumbled on. The plane didn't feel right, but it was still moving. There was a little ground fire, kind of an after thought almost."

Billy gets up and pours himself another drink.

"There were warning lights all over the place…then Luke said,

'I've got control, the engines are running. What's the heading?'

"I said,

'Hold 330, should…'

'I'VE GOT THE LIGHTS! 11 o'clock,' Luke yells and turns toward the light and he starts descending, like he wants to go right into it.

'Watch your altitude!' I shout at Luke.

"I'm worried that he's fixated, but he levels and we make the drop right on the flares that whoever the fuck was down there had lit for us. It was the blackest spot of all... Then Luke pulled it up and away through the clouds, and into the clear night.

"I remember looking around for the Mig that should have been there, given our luck. But Luke has more realistic problems on his mind. He's calling the tanker. We had 2,800 pounds of fuel, which meant 28 minutes until flame out. The plane was shuddering, didn't want to fly right but it wouldn't quit either. The tanker guys got us a vector and the tanker pilot told us he was heading towards us.

I ask Billy.

"Those tanker guys had some cahones. Did they press into the North to find you?"

Billy explains, "If they hadn't we would've had to punch out over who knows what. Luke was having trouble flying it until we slowed to three hundred or so, then it seemed to agree to stay in the air. We decided to turn the damn lights on and screw the Migs that might find us. We needed the tanker and there wasn't time or fuel to miss the connection. Ironically, what might have saved us was the radar. It still worked in air-to-air mode and I found the gas boys and we headed straight assed at them. They turned their lights on, too, and it was a beautiful sight. You know, Oliver, those guys hit the turn perfect. We told them our speed and they did a 180 and we slid right in behind. Luke was working his ass off to get on the boom. We were wallowing; the boom operator was trying to help. You know how the hook looks on a normal rejoin? How it's right above the backseat right on the other side of the canopy. I used to think what would happen if the thing snapped through. That night it was ten times worse. I could feel that fucker smashing my skull. Then Luke decided to blow the tip tanks. There was a warning light and he figured they maybe weren't right. It seemed to help the wallowing. I think one of them was hit and bled off its fuel. Somehow, after that we hooked. Less than ten minutes until flameout. I remember Luke saying,

"Tanker, can you plot us a course for Korat? We need to get this thing on the ground as quickly as possible.'

"We took 6,000 pounds. That was an hour more. We figured being lighter on landing was better.

"The tanker guys were like a big mother hen. They sensed what we'd been through and you could feel their concern. The aircraft commander said they were waiting for us at Korat, with emergency gear standing by.

"Luke tells the whole tanker crew that they're fantastic and it's a true mutual respect thing."

Billy pauses and I think that there was nobility of effort at times - when a tanker would come into heavier air space with no defense at all, or when a guy would press lower on a bombing run so he wouldn't hit civilians, or when the choppers would hover over bad fire to save someone.

Billy continues,

"Here was our status when we left the tanker. Several warning lights, including utility hydraulics, intermittent fire warning, and partial electrical failure. There were some others I can't remember, but I can remember the shuddering that continued and seemed to be getting worse.

"We got Korat on the horn and they tell us the weather. They were at 400 to 500 feet and a mile and a half visibility and light rain, but the winds were calm. That might save us. Luke man, what a job he did on that approach. He blew the gear down early, trying to get trimmed and on the glide slope. He kept saying,

'I can't hold it.'

"Just when it would feel like it was going to stall or just go out of control, Luke would push up the power, and the thing would stabilize a little. The flaps would not come down, so you know it was a fast approach, about 160 knots. All I could do was hang on and keep one hand on the stick, and the other one on the ejection handle. God, I hated the back fucking seat."

Billy pauses...and I put out my hand to him. His hand is clammy and cold. I wish now that I could have given him more comfort. I wish I could have told him this shit that happened was super weird and we both needed to cry and scream, anything but this fucking male constrictive. I wish he were here now.

"We broke out at 400 feet and Luke got it on, but you could feel the extra speed. No brakes but the drag chute came out and even then we rolled a hell of long way. We actually hit the first barrier on the other end.

"Luke and I got the hell out of there. I remember standing on the wings, watching the rescue trucks roll up, thinking it can't be over."

I realize now that it wasn't over for Billy. It would never be over for him.

Never.

"One of the drivers, a sergeant, said something about the plane not looking too good. There were holes in the tail, in the ailerons, and afterburner cans. The thing looked tired, shot up and tired."

"I shook Luke's hand. He patted me on the shoulder.

We didn't talk. It was beyond talk, that moment.

"One of the airmen said there was a flight shack over off the runway, and we walked over. I started getting very cold. You know that feeling you get after a bad ride, like you don't have body warmth? Everything's just flat and empty, sort of.

"Anyway when we opened the door there was a 105 jock sitting behind a desk with a superior attitude.

'Where are you guys from?

"Luke said,

'Da Nang. F-4's'

"The guy kind of sneered and said,

'What do you want out of me?'"

Now it's important to understand the relationship between the 105 pilots and the F-4 crews.

The 105 is a single seat machine. Impressive in some ways, limited in others, it was the only one pilot machine that could survive big strikes around Hanoi. Or at least that was the conventional wisdom. The guys that flew it considered it the ultimate warrior lance. Some of them were cool, some arrogant, some real assholes. The assholes, one of which Billy had encountered in that lonely flight shack, thought the F-4, what with two whole beings in it, was not cool enough, not existential enough, a second rate gig.

Many of them believed that the 105s jocks were the true studs. Just ask guys like this one.

Billy continues,

"The Thud guy actually goes back to reading a book, as we stood there trying to deal with him. Then the phone rang, which kind of shocked all of us. The guy picks it up and then he bolts upright in his chair and says,

'Yes, sir, they're right here…Yes, Sir, General.'

"He hands Luke the phone. Luke says,

'Yes sir, General Westmoreland. It was successful. Yes sir, it was a little hairy. Yes sir. Thank you sir. You want us to come to Saigon now? We'll try to catch a plane…oh, well if you want to send your plane that would be…thanks again.'

"Luke hands the phone back to our pal.

'The Thud guy doesn't say anything. He just reaches under the desk and pulls out a bottle of Wild Turkey and three glasses. He sits them in front of us and gets us chairs. We drank in silence.'"

CHAPTER 32

The Justice of it All

Billy Parris stood with his combat medal folders clutched to his chest, weaving and sweating. Dulove, his lawyer, who made me want to throw up, looked bored and was trying to get Billy to plead guilty. It was obvious the sleaze hadn't done anything on the case.

"Look Mr. Parris I think you should just plead guilty and hope for a first offense low end sentence."

"I…I…don't want to. I wa…want t…to…here, give these to the uh, judge."

Billy pushes the folders at this fuck. I didn't even want Dulove to touch them, and apparently this representative of the bar felt the same. He recoiled, pushing the awards back at Wil, keeping his hands open-unwilling to clasp that which he couldn't possibly really gather.

"Look, these are irrelevant and might bother the judge…"

He pauses and looks at Billy, suddenly uncertain of what's going on here.

Again the folders are thrust at him; forceful like an old man, angry and shaking.

"Ju...st show him, dammit."

There's a dangerous gleam in Billy's eye.

Hopeful for better results, Dulove turns toward me.

I figure Billy's wrong, myself, but I ain't showing this clown anything. Wil's suffering has had little enough impact. I'm here to lie for him-swear he wasn't drunk when he left my pad in south Miami. Actually he was ripped, wasted. He had been medically retired at 28 and completely shredded after the Da Nang dance. Long before PTSD had found itself into the vocabulary of war damage, Billy was its embodiment. He had come over one night to visit ghosts with me. Our ghosts, shared since the tour together in Viet Nam, flew around the room as we went over the loss of 28 F-4 Phantom's in our wing. 56 aviators were caught, killed, drowned, or recovered.

"We will drink to those who gave their all of old, then down we roar to score the rainbow's pot of gold."

Billy and I sang that song at the Air Force Academy. The fucking pot of gold never came our way but we sure did drink to giving your all, and looking at Billy looking at me it maybe means more than exploding or drowning or burning or being tortured to death in a hole in Laos.

"Here's a toast to the host of those who love the vastness of the sky."

To me at that point 'vastness' applies in a horrific sense to the extension of the killing ground upwards. You know that 'long delirious burning blue' can be grabbed more than one way.

We killed and were killed and we came 'screaming from the sky' to do it. Now my friend was standing in front of a 'successful' professional trying to keep his nervous system from completely shattering itself. Trying to talk, trying to stand so he can be judged.

Dulove shrugs with condescension, takes the folders and in we go.

It was the first time I'd ever been in a courtroom and the majesty, God, the majesty of it all. This superior being in flowing robes was looking down from a desk the building of which must have taken the destruction of twenty trees. It was impressive. And the altitude difference between the bench and the rest of us was wonderful. From up high, it is easier to vanquish your foe, come out of the blazing sun of constitutional righteousness.

Just like a good fighter pilot, a judge never gives up the height advantage.

The cop who nailed Billy stands looking straight ahead and the farce begins. It's funny how he never looked at Billy. But then the meat cutter never notices a particular slab of beef. It's all just meat.

"He was weaving; he was starting and stopping; he was incoherent…"

While the prosecutor was eliciting this testimony from the blue suit, the judge was doing an interesting thing. He was engrossed in the medal descriptions. His head leaned forward; he seemed to go into them. The only time he looked up was to stare at Billy.

The state rested.

I tried to help, when Dulove asked me about that night.

"He was fine when he left my…" I lied.

The judge never looked up, just kept reading.

The eyes of the authority finally look down.

"Mr. Parris, I find you guilty of driving under the influence. You were a danger to the safety of the streets of Miami."

The judge paused and looked around the scene. He raised his volume and says,

"This man holds the Silver Star, 3 distinguished Flying crosses, 15 Air medals…"

He looked at my comrade with respect. Wil fidgeted, glanced with eyes half there at the speaker of his praise, glanced at Dulove, and then looked at me. In that look was anger and pride and confusion and a hint of death. In that look was a universe of species longing and species hate and species love.

"If this court can offer mercy to anyone, it can offer it to this man. This sentence is adjudicated. Mr. Parris, this means you can go. There is no sanction."

Wil jerked his head to his lawyer and said.

"Ge...get my me..dals"

Dulove walks up to the judge and receives them. He looks like an alter boy as he carries them back to Wil.

Wil Parris takes them, spins on his heel in the best Academy tradition and walks slowly out, clutching his books like a shy schoolgirl. Everyone in the joint is looking at him.

"See, Dulove, I told you. I...I told you."

It was the last time I ever saw him. He drank himself to death some years later.

What I didn't realize or admit was how much he was to me and I to him.

What I didn't acknowledge was the judge was me and I him.

What I didn't admit was the whole fucking system had suffered and there was some halting groping compassion for the stricken ones.

To John Gillespie McGee

Yeah I've pulled the bastard screaming into the air

and raged the rent on serious edges

and watched the wing light blinking me follow

through pitch that bumped my spine awake

I've launched erect rockets and

fell off interrupted and fell off glad

with mad raging power shoving me up through light that loses

its earthly gleam

i've pulled through rectitudes of air

and swirled the sky as sea as sky

It encompassed me with hallowed hardness

and shot my being with joy and solitude

About the Author

Ron Oliver, a 1965 United States Air Force Academy Graduate was pre-humorously awarded a Distinguished Flying Cross, 13 Air Medals, and several standard military medals for his tour at Da Nang Air Force Base in South Vietnam from 1967-1968.

He was also awarded a bad case of PTSD (Post Traumatic Stress Disorder) and an Article 15. After escaping the Air Force, Oliver worked as a preschool dishwasher, golf ball diver, truck driver, gardener, light airplane aerial photography pilot, and other things he's forgotten or repressed. He lives with no cats or dogs in Healdsburg, California.

Glossary

AFA The Air Force Academy. It was also known as the "blue zoo" or just the "zoo."

Article 15 Part of the uniform code of military justice. A disciplinary judgment in lieu of a court-martial, rarely given to officers.

Bingo When an aircraft has minimum fuel remaining. Time to hit a tanker or head home.

backseaters The F-4 pilot who was not in control, in the backseat of the plane.

B-36 Huge bomber using 10 engines, 6 turbo props, and 4 jets; never used in the Vietnam War.

Blue zoo Air Force Academy

Breaking out Climbing above a cloud layer/overcast weather that is clearing

C-130s Four-engine turbo prop cargo plane.

cbu's Cluster bomb units were a vicious weapon consisting of a large canister, which, after being dropped deploys hundreds of smaller bomb units, each containing hundreds of steel balls capable of completely annihilating a large area.

DFC Distinguished Flying Cross. The Distinguished Flying Cross is a medal awarded to an officer or enlisted member of the United States armed forces for extraordinary service in the air.

DMZ. Demilitarized Zone is a small stretch of land ostensibly separating North and South Vietnam.

dogfighting Aerial Combat between fighter aircrafts. The term originated during World War I when pilots had to switch off their engines to avoid turning into the torque, and then restart them, which from the ground sounded like dogs barking.

FAC Forward Air Controllers are small prop planes used for spotting targets. They could be prickly if attacked, which the North Vietnamese knew and often didn't shoot at them. Let sleeping FACs lie, so to speak.

F-80/F-86 Early jet fighters featured in the Korean War.

F-100 First supersonic fighter circa late 1950s to late 1960s

flak Detritus or debris from exploding anti aircraft shells.

Frontseaters The F-4 pilot who was in control in the front of the plane.

g's Gravitational units. 1 g is the normal gravitational pull. 2 g's is twice the normal gravitational pull and so on.

GCA Ground Controlled Approach was used to talk F-4s down in bad weather.

Gut check An evaluation of one's current bravery or determination

ILS Instrument Landing System was a more advanced system where the pilot flies two electronic beams (horizontal and vertical) to the runway. The F-4s didn't have this necessity because the Navy couldn't use it on carriers and the F-4 was a Navy design.

inertial nav An internal navigation system based on gyroscopes, mechanisms that aid direction but didn't always work very well.

jinking Rapidly changing altitude and heading, much like a drunken bird in order to throw off the anti - craft gunners.

karst These are nasty grey, jagged, razor sharp mountain formations in Laos. It was my opinion that they were the worst possible stuff to eject over, especially since the Pathet Lao rebels were even more vicious than the Viet Cong NVA consortium.

Lead Short for leader in a fighter formation. All radio talk is designed for brevity.

Marconi Slang for radio.

Migs These are Russian fighter planes that were used by North Vietnam. The Mig 21 was their primary ride. During the Korean War the Mig 15 was the model used.

NVA The North Vietnamese Army.

O-2 The Air Forces main spotter plane in Vietnam. It was a pusher puller prop plane.

OER Officer Efficiency Reports are the mechanisms by which each officer rates a junior officer for promotion merit. Like an inflated grade rank in school, it was normal to get high OER's, thus rendering them meaningless unless one received a bad one.

PAC One North Vietnam was partitioned into seven areas or PACs for control purposes by US command. PAC One was the one at the southern end.

Pickle Pushing a small red button on the flight control stick causing bombs to fall.

Pipper Small dot on targeting windscreen.

Punch To push through a cloud deck

Punch out To eject from the airplane

RAF The Royal Air Force was the British air arm. They did not fly in Vietnam.

SAC Strategic Air Command.

Sams Surface to Air Missiles were made by the Russians and installed in North Vietnam

Sapper Infiltrating, often suicidal, combatants who carried explosives strapped to their bodies.

Thud F-105 Thunder Chief shortened to thud.

Two Short for the wingman in a fighter formation. All radio talk is designed for brevity.

Tanker Boeing converted to an air-to-air refueler C-135

37s 37 millimeter anti aircraft

57s 57 millimeter anti aircraft

750s Seven hundred fifty pound bombs.

20 mm center line gatling gun A detachable cigar-shaped 20-millimeter gun with rotating barrels. The gun was capable of firing 4,000 to 6,000 rounds per minute. It was hung like a bomb under the fuselage of the F-4.